HOLD ON
AND DIE

OR

LET GO
AND LIVE

Pastor Mac

ISBN: 9781736102855

WEBSTER'S DICTIONARY VS BIBLICAL INTERPRETATION

WEBSTERS

Death: The permanent, irreversible cessation of all biological functions that sustain a living organism.

BIBLICAL (you shall surely die)

Death: A slow, painful and hard loss, depleting, deteriorating and diminishing quality of life

(Genesis 3)

WEBSTERS

Life: The quality that distinguishes a vital and functional being from a dead body

BIBLICAL

Life: Abundant, long, peaceful, joy, good health, prosperity, hope and a sound mind

THE POWER OF LIFE AND DEATH IS IN THE TONGUE
(Proverbs 18:21)

And they that love it shall eat the fruit thereof.

The ability to act or produce an effect.

CHOOSE LIFE (Deuteronomy 30:19)

You get to say, live or accept the conditions of the one you choose

Contents:

Introduction

T he philosophies that I started out with at the age of 16, when I wrote my mother a three-page letter as to why I was leaving the home and dropping out of school were honorable and seemingly appropriate. At each interval (crossroad), my teachers became disenchanting, they showed no great interest and patience with challenging students and understanding their socio-economic foundation. All too often I heard, "I got mine." School was serving no purpose for me or what I believe was a driving force in my life. I felt like I could learn more "in the streets" or on the job training. My father of eight children, was a forty-nine-year alcoholic who we had to sometimes rescue from the street two times a day. He beat my mother and left many permanent scars in her heart and on her body. She stayed with him and took his punishment because of her eight children. Before his demise from colon cancer in 2000 he met Christ and changed his life and became a deacon of the church and a self-trained electrician who worked at

Howard University. I will share more in Chapter one.

As a result of his relationship at Howard University, he was able to send one of his eight children to college. We were on "welfare" before it became more eloquently called "public assistance." We received powdered milk. Not Jif Peanut Butter, but USDA 10356 and not Welch's grape jelly, but USDA 30633 was its name. This program later advanced to a more acceptable "food stamp" program and not so embarrassing, an EBT card. In my life at the age of 16 I started out looking for a better way. I left home to be an example to my mother and to prove to her that life could be better for us. I wanted to show her by my accomplishments that our conditions and lifestyle were not her fault. At her present age of 89 she has outlived my father of 49 years of alcoholism, who followed the social lifestyle as his father did. Also, she has outlived a 15-year relationship with a longtime friend who died a very stubborn and rebellious life of a severe diabetic. In his most severe condition, he was hardheaded and disobedient to the rapidly failing causes of diabetes; excessive sugar intake. In many cases small puddles of water drained from his legs and feet in a matter of 10-15 minutes. Close to his final deterioration when she felt that she could not help him, she called and asked me to please come and remove him from her home to take him somewhere that could help him. As a veteran, I took him to the Red Clinic Veterans Affairs (VA) Medical Center in Washington, D.C.. They told me that they could not help him. I told them that it was their responsibility to help him and I was not taking him back to my mother's home where he lived. They accused me of being inconsiderate and uncaring, and questioned "what kind of preacher would do this to someone." Being held accountable for others' responsibilities (The VA) and accused of others (my mother's friend) for issues and mismanagement of their lives was simply a continuation of the path my life encompassed. I left him at the VA. My mother's friend of 35 years. before their courtship, in my sincere attempt to love him and help him, accused me of abandoning him. Of all the people he told me, I never thought you would do this to me. I genuinely felt that I had disappointed the man that I loved, respected and was determined to help. He died of a severe and debilitating case of diabetes three days later. My mother asked me and further placed the responsibility of his care in my hands, and I had to live with someone leaving this earth accusing me of their fate and at worst questioning my ethical behavior as a pastor representing God.

My mother also survived three sons, Darryl, Tony, and Michael. Michael was killed in a 50 MPH head on collision on his way home for Thanksgiving in 1984.The driver of the car that my brother was in, died on impact. Five hours later, Prince George's Hospital in Maryland released my brother to go home. Unknowingly, due to the level of their urgent care he had a ruptured spleen, three broken ribs and was bleeding internally. We drove him home not realizing that he was dying. He almost collapsed while I carried him into the home. Two hours later, lying on my mother's bed, he started crying out," I can't breathe", rolling from side to side as I sat alone with him. Both legs started getting cold and ultimately, he died on the way to Howard University Hospital. My mother was given tranquilizers after we were told "we couldn't save him" and she lost her memory for the next seven days. I attributed this to God covering her mind and protecting her from what was about to kill her, losing her first child. She later asked me if there was anything I could have done to save or help him while taking him into the house. The question shattered my spirit and my inability to help her at the darkest hour of her life. If I had known of his internal condition, I would have put him back in the car and drove him to Howard University Hospital. To this day, I have not answered her question and the guilt that I have carried for something someone else did not do. Caring for something, and taking responsibility for something that is not mine has plagued my life.

She is also survived by my brother Tony, who was shot in the head on New Year's Eve of 1988. His head was swollen and looked like an exact replica of ET. Not being able to see him anymore was a message I had to carry to my mom from the mortician. Her instruction to me was "go take care of my son." When calls and visits came in, many would ask in their conceivable concern for her mourning, "what happened", which would send her deeper into her pain and confusing ability to think clearly. At one point I said, "Mother, you don't have to think and remember, I'll think for you, I will be your mind." My brother was a hustler and my mother shared with me how she would lay many nights sleepless, worried and wondering like so many mothers when she would get the call.

The year of 1988 was the highest homicide rate in the District of Columbia (573 murders), and he was the last one. My mother often shared a concern with me, how people would perceive her not mourning her son. She confided in me that the call represented a relief from worry and anxiety now knowing finally where her son was and that he was no longer in danger. Her expectations of me, unnoticed and unappreciated by my siblings, was a revelation and clear reflection of the path my life was taking. Lastly, my mother is survived by my oldest brother, Darryl. I

took my brother Darryl to identify my brother Tony's body with one-fourth of his head missing and swollen by the impact and trauma of the gunshot. It was overwhelming and too much to envision. The site was so devastating that Darryl went into a depressive state, deep isolation and excessive drug use. Eight months later he was found in a saltwater sea in Norfolk, Virginia. He was swollen from the salt and fish had picked and punctured his body each time tearing his flesh. The body bag could not be opened and he was identified by dental records. This brought to a close, the constant requests to check up on him, and find him, when I hadn't heard from him, to make sure he was okay.

So, as I begin to share my life's story which encompasses the beginning of my 50-year journey, you will be able to detect the driving force that compelled the nine chapters of my life and all of the intricate experiences therein. You will be able to see the foundation of my pursuit to live better, be better, and prove to my mother that her faultless sacrifices are hinged on her many expectations of me. That my convictions (firmly held beliefs), my commitment(dedication), and my compassion (sympathetic concern for the sufferings and misfortunes of others) would result in condemnation, criticism and conflict from and by those who directly and extensively benefited from me. Little did I know when I started this journey in life that at every turn, every relationship, every business, every church and marriage would result in me giving so much of myself to others and receiving so little from others to the point of my demise and sufferings. They turned my good into evil. Psalms 35:12 -15 says *"they rewarded me evil for my good to the spoiling of my soul"* NIV. As for me, when they were sick, my clothing was a sackcloth. I humbled my soul with fasting; and my prayer turned into my own bosom. I behaved myself as though he had been my brother or friend; I bowed down heavily as one that mourned for his mother, but in my adversity, they rejoiced, and gathered themselves together; yea, the abjects gathered themselves together against me and I knew it not; they did tear me, and ceased not."

I will share more in Chapters 3 and 6---.

Lord, how long wilt thou look on? Rescue my soul from their destruction. The challenges or questions I faced in each instance and ultimately faced after 50 years of living all rested upon God's freedom of choice. Proverbs 18:21 says that the power of life and death is in the tongue. Choose life and not death. The questions that have consistently embodied my fate at every turn involve, in essence, making a conscientious decision to live or die. How long do I allow you to contribute to my death or demise? How long do I allow or tolerate pain, pressure and problems for the sake of love or duty and responsibility to my fellow man? How much do I have to lose, struggle or suffer for someone or something else because of their selfish and inconsiderate misguided expectations? How long do I choose to let you depreciate, deplete and diminish the quality of Abundant Life that God ordained for me in Jeremiah 29:11? "For I know the plans that I have for you; they are plans for good and not for disaster, to give you a future and a hope, an expected end. How long do I allow your need for me or expectations of me, to cripple me and incarcerate me? When do I let go and let God or when do I let go and live and realize that as long as I hold onto this stronghold over my life or this hot coal, it's going to scorch, severely

burn (ruin) or scar me permanently? As long as I hold on or attach myself to your issues. I will never be able to live out the true quality and purpose promised or available to me also. It will destroy my pursuit of life, liberty and pursuit of happiness. Hold on and die or let go and live.

I needed to understand the true meaning and appropriate interpretation of death and life. I found it in Genesis 2:17. The free will to accept and enjoy (partake of) the good and the evil and the self-imposed consequences of both. It states there that " of every tree of the garden, you may eat: But of the tree of the knowledge of Good and Evil, Thou shalt not eat of it: for in the day (moment, era, process of time) that thou eatest thereof. Thou shalt surely die. It is clear from this choice, death as pronounced or promised didn't mean stop breathing or cease to exist any longer. We were created to live forever. We made a choice and the conditions and quality of our lives changed immediately. As a result of that choice we began to suffer, sweat, hurt and experience difficulty in health. We did not change or correct that choice and the length of life decreased. The choice changed the length, quality, substance and purpose. In essence death was pronounced and the length of life followed this reality. Forever became 125 years, and later threescore and ten years which is 70. Twenty represents a score. Life after 70 years was a result of God's favor or kindness beyond what is due or earned.

Subsequently, death means the slow depletion, deterioration, draining, and diminishing of the quality of life we were created to live. Long, perfect, painless, productive, peaceful and plenteous were the characteristics that governed or defined our creation. Every day and in every situation in life we have the ability through our choices to reverse the curse, increase and enhance the quality, substance and value of our lives. To rightly divide(interpret and apply) God's expectations of us and our duty to the kingdom as Christians is to do what Kenny Rogers sang about, " You got to know when to hold them, know when to fold them, know when to pick them up and when to put them down". He applied this intricate process of life to a simple card game.

But the enemy, through his agents and supporters, some of which are in your family, church members, your BFFs, coworkers and friends like leeches, fleas, and ticks through envy, jealousy and fear comes like a thief in the night when you least expect it for the purpose of stealing killing and destroying. They attach themselves to you and catch you off-guard when you're weak. They rob you of the quality of life you desire and of the abundant and overcoming life that Jesus secured on the cross. He is shrewd in entangling and entrapping us into philosophies, and beliefs and has us convinced into believing that it is of God, The Holy Spirit and in the name of Christ. He did it in the garden with Adam and Eve by convincing them that God didn't really say what he meant and didn't really mean what he said. He sets us up to kill us, drain us, and to distract and deceive us into thinking something is not what it is. He misdirects us for his own personal agenda and game. Who was convinced that the work that I was doing was for God and to some degree, I still am. I was committed and deeply engaged and on many occasions told that I was a Godsend, an angel, as I consumed my time energy and money deeply depriving myself of life abundantly for people who are selfish, ungrateful, insensitive, egotistical, self-centered and it was literally killing me and blessing them.

I will share more in Chapter 4---

The loss of a 25-year marriage, the loss of a church that I pastored and founded for 15 years, blood pressure up to 205 /183, severe weight loss, stabbing me in the back, smiling in my face, draining all of my financial resources, destroying my credibility, using me on every level was in fact, defeating, depleting, and diminishing. In the words of Roberta Flack "Killing Me Softly". This was in fact, in addition to all of my physical challenges. I was stabbed a fraction of an inch from my heart, cirrhosis of the liver, Hepatitis C for 44 years, high blood pressure, diabetes, sciatica, enlarged prostate, heart murmur, chronic kidney disease, blocked artery in my neck, double and walking pneumonia, both which were deadly. But I was obedient to my profession as a Christian and pastor who instructed me in Christ's Sermon on the Mount, Matthew 5:44," but I say unto you, love your enemies, bless them that curse you, do good to them that hate you, and pray for them which despitefully use you and persecute you". I love Jesus who is the" author and finisher of my faith," To a fault. I needed clear answers. I needed to hear directly from him but all I had to depend on was" His word". Where do I draw the line? How much do I take? How long do I hold on to what is literally draining life and hope from me daily? It is destroying everything I put my hands to, every business, every church and every marriage. Seemingly, I gave it all, expecting nothing in return. But in every major area of my life I suffered loss and ultimate failure from the beginning at age 16 and a vast majority of 50 years. I was trapped (or called) into doing good, being good and caring more for others than I did for myself, no matter what it cost me. Be an example and esteem others above yourself.

I will share more in Chapters 2, 3, and 9---

Because of my sincere love for Jesus and the extreme sacrifices I strongly believe he made for me, since I met Jesus, I've been driven and compelled to reciprocate his actions and be guided by His words and instructions no matter how much I had to sacrifice or suffer and deep in my inner being, that is my soul. I was still determined to show and prove to my mother that all of the sacrifices that she made for me and her children were not in vain and that the choices that we made as adults should not solely define the success of her sacrifices and the quality of her ability as a mother.

I met Jesus in 1980 when I lost my first marriage.

I will share more in Chapter 1---

The story of the Cross gripped my soul and has never waned. To phantom the concept that someone could love you so much that they would not only endure unbearable, extreme suffering and sacrifices, but would literally die for you was etched in my spirit immediately. I connected. As a result, my relationship has been literal and with no gray areas and real. NAIVE I MAY BE. It has been indelibly permeated in my soul like super glue. The gospel song possibly written by Fanny Crosby in 1869 and so eloquently performed by the famous Mississippi Mass Choir is recorded like this:

Jesus keep me near the Cross, there's a precious fountain

Free to all a healing stream flows from Calvary's Mountain.

Near the Cross a trembling soul, love and mercy found me

There the Bright and Morning Star shed its beams around me

Near The Cross oh Lamb of God, bring its scenes before me.

Help me walk from day to day, with its shadows over me.

 Near the Cross I will watch and wait, hoping trusting ever

Till I reach that golden strand, just beyond the river.

Near the Cross, near the Cross, be my glory ever

Till my raptured soul shall find, rest beyond the river.

These words and his love for me has captured my very being and embodies the very profound effect it has on me every time I activate my vocal cords to sing it, I get choked up and overwhelmed with tears. Oh, how I love Jesus. In my search over the years for an answer to the question, when is it appropriate to simply let go and let God? Easily said and often used as a scapegoat for avoiding responsibility, escaping the mandate we have as Christians in particular, Christian leadership. However, our convictions won't let us walk away and give up on people or situations because Christ even while we were still sinning (doing wrong and messing up) did not give up on us. But the question remains...

How much do I give? How much do I tolerate? How long do I allow situations to consume me to my own destruction and despair? How long do I hold on (dying in value, substance and quality)? And when do I let go of what's financially, spiritually, socially and psychologically crushing my will to live? Let go, drop this hot coal that's deteriorating my flesh, this weight that's suppressing my ability to thrive, move, rise up and live? When do I let go of carrying you and your stuff so that I can flow in the fulfillment of my own? I realized a form of measurement that helps me grapple with this dilemma by applying this question in all things that I undertake. What would Jesus do? It entails glorifying God, sharing his love and empowers me to endure hardship like a good soldier and escape the deceptive and destructive fiery darts of the enemy before all too often suffering damaging results. For doing good, they killed him, as an Under Shepherd, what should I expect and what is really required of me?

As a preacher and pastor since 1984, I was constantly reminded that Christ died for us. As His agent, image, and Under Shepherd, I was obligated to live out in all things His devotion to lives and commitment to suffer for others. So, I measured every situation in my life to that defining question and proverbial expression: what would Jesus do?" Die? Live? Suffer? I was reminded by a colleague of mine periodically of a word in Colossians 3:23, "Do what you know to do". Today, as I write this book, after 50 years of suffering a light begins to shine out the answer found in Romans 12:18.: If it be possible, as much as lieth in you to do, live peaceably with all men". Matthew Henry in his commentary on Romans 12:16 wrote this: this united love and being of the same mind one towards another. labor, as much as you can, to agree in apprehension and wherein you come short of this, yet agree in affection; Endeavour to

be all one, not affecting to clash, and contradict, and thwart one another: but keep the unity of the spirit in the bond of peace. Philemon 2:2 and 3:15.

Through my life, I assert to you, that it seems evident that God understands our human frailties and boundaries, limitations and thresholds. You've heard that it is hard to love some people and even though instructed by God to do so: impossible to love and embrace others. This concept in Romans 12:16 further implies to me that there is a place in all of us that meets that end to "God will put no more on us than we can bear" or through the disconnected aspects of reality that Dr. King spoke of "are capable of bearing".

When we question how much more is required of me, there seems to be a clear distinction that at some point we must draw a line. A place and time where retreating is appropriate. A place and a time where I have lived out God's expectations of me in this matter. A time to give the sacrifice that I made an opportunity to come into fruition or work out the purpose for which I was used to serving. And now I must let go and allow the sacrifices and contributions I've made to flourish or fail in others, knowing I've done my best and keep it moving without retaliatory retribution for detaching. That day has come in my 50 years as an adult from the age of 16. Results were not appreciated or received and reciprocated favorably. My results, as they often have, doesn't imply failure (a more positive end). But simply denotes that I've given all I was assigned in the nine chapters of my life and must move on. (let go and let God), only if I have been faithful in my duty to serve. It is important here to note in Romans 12:15 to 16, that every good and perfect gift comes from God. Every level of wisdom and insight, the ability to have and do comes from God. Every calling, responsibility and accomplishment comes from above (God).

The best and most useful man on the planet is no more or no better than what God's grace and mercy has awarded him in Romans 12:16, I find the ultimate conclusion to the whole matter. The ultimate role in our lives as Christians. The ultimate duty required in our assigned or chosen roles to our family, friends or foes or to those we have been given the privilege to serve is this: Micah 6:8, "he has shown you O mortal, what is good and what does the Lord require of you? To do justly, and to love mercy, and to walk humbly with your God." Rejoice when others rejoice and weep when others weep. That's what I was told, and that's what I did. Bear one another's burdens, not carry their cross. That's what I was told and that's what I did. Condescend to men of low estate (be reachable and meet people at their needs. That's what I was told, and that's what I did. Love your enemy, those who hate and use you, pray for them (in spite of). That's what I was told and that's what I did. Give to others what you expect others to give to you. That's what I was told and that's what I did. Inasmuch as it is in you to do, live peaceably with all men. God gives you what you have the ability to do. Do all that you are humanly capable of, with the resources life has awarded you and know when you've done all that is ultimately required to do.

Today, I have applied these instructional mandates in all nine major areas of my existence and desire at every instance and operating (managing) under constant pressure and undue hardship has resulted in the theme of this book...

Hold on and Die or Let Go and Live.

Holding on to something that is no longer mine to do has contributed to my present fate. Holding onto something and some people who are no longer on my "list of things to do today", or not in my sphere. Holding onto things, people, concepts that are no longer under my chosen or assigned duty is what became draining. Ecclesiastes Chapter 3 says that there is a time and a season for every purpose. I was holding on to things that were out of season and no longer my purpose to fulfill. They were out of timing now and began to cause an adverse effect on the quality of life I was promised and deserved. Like Adam and Eve, I was eating and partaking of a substance that would slowly deteriorate, deplete, and diminish the quality of my life. Killing me softly. I was experiencing a physical, spiritual and emotional death. Test taken, assignment completed, it was now like holding onto a hot coal and justifying why I shouldn't let it go while it's burning the hell out of my hand and leaving me permanently scarred. In my understanding of what death meant (you shall surely die, not a literal death (final existence) but a deterioration of the quality of life we were originally created to live. Consumed by a decrease in longevity, struggle, hard work, sweat, suffering, I saw a new light. I found that confirming doctrine in the institution of marriage and every format used by clergy which includes "till death do us part." The premise is that once you are married, you're in it until you die. The institution of marriage exemplifies God's unfailing, unending an unconditional love that he has with man. I understand that this premise represents a lifetime decision which is why it should not be entered into lightly.

However, I find it somewhat alarming that God would require me to suffer any kind of abuse outside of my control or ability to endure it.

Even I raised my daughters to wit: Any time that a man exhibits mental, physical, psychological or social abuse towards you, walk, trot or run like hell and don't look back. When someone makes a clear message to you that they will or desire to hurt you in any way it only seems intelligent to get out of their path. Likewise, I find it alarming that God who protects and provides for us would find comfort and leave us in danger. The Mosaic law incorporated provisions that provided rescue elements from those who in fact were in this" till death do you part" environment. The Bible teaches us that even though you enter into this lifetime decision, being unfaithful (having an outside affair), there are conditions that does not mean you are being permanently entrapped and bound by someone's infidelity. It represents and violates the pure and sacred sanctity God has in his relationship with man.

Death in fact, other than in its natural course, rarely means the end, but a serious change or separation in relationships as they once were. Finally in this regard, there is no temptation known to man that God has not already provided him with a way of escape. Rightly dividing, interpreting and applying His words in our lives is essential in determining His intent for us. Two things to consider going forward regarding misconceptions or interpretation:

1. What God hath joined together (or you)

2. Till death do us part (or the quality of life is diminishing, killing you)

People do not always have God's best interest at heart, nor yours. and I do not believe he would require you to be held captive, by his instruction or your Mistakes when others are involved. Proverbs 4:7

says", and with all thy getting, get an understanding". Being or feeling compelled to hold on to what in reality was becoming overwhelmingly deadly and detrimental to my health and well-being was not a divine requirement .Being held down by others and their choices was a Misapplication of God's principles of love and commitment to our fellow man, friends, family or foe. Holding on to what was killing me was not an obligation to please God as I strongly felt. Simply in light of the nature of the vow until l I die.

Hold on and die or let go and live, is an internal hidden struggle and painful contrast and pursuit that many today are quietly experiencing because of a misguided sense of duty It Inhibits them from living bright, happy, peaceful, fulfilling and productive lives in fear of disappointing God or people. Just because they made a vow or a promise when led to believe it was safe and okay to engage and accept. I needed to visit what God had to say about this dilemma and once again I found another answer in Proverbs 18:21. The power of life and death is in the tongue, choose life. and at the appointed or appropriate time reject death and the issues that define it. Hold on and die or let go and live is a matter of life and death. How much do I have to take before I let go? How long do I have to die before I realize that I also have a right to live? How much do I have to give before I expect something in return? How much do I have to give of myself before someone reciprocates? When is it appropriate for me to let go of what I feel bound to hold on to? How long does the quality of my life depreciate while those I help elevate? When do I let go of this hot coal that's causing me permanent damage? When do I realize that as long as I am carrying this weight, my life will not elevate and I will never rise above my present circumstances? How much does the Lord require of me regarding you? What real-time elements have destroyed the quality of life as I envisioned it? What dream has died or been put on hold because of something or somebody else? How much of my future has been erased because of your past? How much more should I sacrifice for an ungrateful, insensitive and inconsiderate attitude? When does my life become a priority?

All of these questions encompassed the last 50 years of my life, 41 as a Christian preacher and pastor with a heart for God from 16 to 66 years old. I trust that sharing the intricate, intimate and deeply personal details will help answer yours. As a pastor for 15 years, and Under shepherd and example of Christ who took upon himself all of our sins and issues, I developed an operating theme of my duty to do likewise. My prayer and position for all whom I led spiritually was" Please forgive me for all of the wrongs others have caused in your life. I sincerely apologize" He took so much of our stuff that it changed his form and appearance. However, I've learned that when helping becomes extreme, it hurts the recipient.

It usually hinders people from owning their own stuff and accepting responsibility for their own actions and the consequences thereof. Maybe it's a part of our human anatomy that we are often prone or possess a sense of obligation to cling to things or people that hurt us. That constantly drains us and pulls us uncomfortably. It is justified in many cases by a feeling of indebtedness. A return maybe, for someone's kind acts or contribution often entraps us and leaves us vulnerable and suspectable to be preyed on, used, and taken advantage of.

There are so many reasons that plague our choices and shift, delay or prolong our ability to change, restructure, redirect, realign, reinvent and

re-evaluate our purpose and agenda:

1. Being responsible
2. Feeling indebted
3. Loyalty
4. Fear of being alone
5. Fear of acceptance or rejection
6. Fear of the unknown
7. Fear of failure
8. Self-esteem
9. Pattern
10. Dependency
11. Familiarity
12. Complacency
13. A need to be validated by others
14. Fear of Starting Over Again

All of these categories are crippling and cause death. A need to be validated by others that results in us tolerating their treatment and behavior toward us. They are defeating and they limit the quality-of-life God desires and his creation deserves. They deteriorate and diminish the quality of life we can live. We often Justify, make excuses or accept what others want and not what we deserve. When we do this, we actually disappoint God who wants so badly for us to live in the abundance of life, unbarred or hinged by Satan's tactics of failure and disillusionment.

He deceives, distracts, distorts, and he steals, kills and destroys hopes and dreams. Which category are you? Where do you presently find yourself? What has blocked your path to life, liberty and the pursuit of happiness? What are you holding on to that is constantly crushing your potential and ability to choose life and not death? To live and not die? Prosper and not perish?

It is my sincere desire that through my life's lessons, the nine major chapters of my life that you will find that place. That time or need to examine the quality of life that God gave you, or the quality of life that has been taken away from you. It is my sincere desire that you would visit the offer that my experiences are inviting and help encourage you to decide whether to Hold on and Die or Let go and Live

Chapter 1

16-17 Years Old

My life started in real time when I left home at 16. All of my reasons for leaving were good and honorable intentions to be better, successful and a contribution to society and not a detriment. They were not the typical drugs, sex, alcohol, babies and Rebellion against my parents, but they soon developed into all-out war and against everything, I desired to be. There was seemingly an immediate attack on my identity. An attack on my character and foundation and purpose. An invisible, hidden force and strategy to destroy me. Everything that I touched or strived to accomplish was met with adverse opposition. It was a force working against me, my identity and my compassionate heart. An evil agenda. As far back as I can remember, I dreamed of flying, soaring in the air. It often felt like I was in a cage trying to find and fight my way out and never could rise. Just climbing up and gliding through the air. Funny as it is, my name is Arnold and it represents an eagle. Don't know if my parents were aware of that. My name means "Eagle - power - soaring". It is America's bird. But in my dreams sometimes I would run but could never lift up and fly, kind of like pulling a kite that always falls down. Sometimes I was able, through some invisible force, to lift up but I could never soar. There was always something or somebody pulling me down or pulling at me. Hindering me and interrupting my flow. It was like having oil on my wing weighing me down or being in a vacuum. A vicious unending cycle. Every business, marriage, and church in my life, fits this criteria. Always some explosive element or expectation planted to corrupt, destruct, deceive, deplete, deteriorate and diminish the quality of life I desired to live, purpose and assignments I attempted to accomplish. I strived as a measure in all of my actions to do all to the glory of God and in all things please him. That resulted in me doing everything well and with an acknowledgment and praise. But even in that they returned me evil for my good works. The first immediate attack when I left home seemed to be on my identity, character and nature. In hindsight, believing I was called to be a pastor, my first encounter was with a pastor, and his all-out agenda was to break me. It was to make me his gay b****, sex doll and puppet by convincing me that he was concerned for me and my youthful dilemma and as a pastor, could and should in his capacity would help me and be there for me. It is so very dangerous to be young and ignorant in America. However, this proved in time not to be the case.

Deception and like fear which is false evidence appearing real, began to unravel. The very nature of who I was, was attacked right out of the gate by a man who claimed to be a representative of the Kingdom of Heaven, of which I was destined to operate. A Christian leader. Shepherd. Man of God. My immediate challenge was to establish my identity, my place in the universe and myself with a determined but divinely directed purpose for living but soon became escaping what someone else wanted me to be. My supposed help became my immediate hurt and started killing who I desired and purposed to be before I even got my footing. Converting me from a young man on a mission to a b****whore, for his sick and perverted pleasure. What a contrast. I needed him now, I had nowhere to go. Hold on and die? He was stealing my life before I could even establish it. A pastor's performance had the potential to influence my passion, and fate and my will to fulfill my call and cause. What a wonderful example for me to follow, right?

Every Sunday morning on the way to church, he would open up his aluminum package of cocaine at a red light and take two to three hits through his nostrils. Surprisingly, preaching his congregation to their feet and highest level of praise and worship, demonstrating the awesome power and love of God. Wow… Whenever he left home, he would leave instructions to this huge man four times my size and weight, to break me, and to by force prepare me and make me surrender to his sexual dominance and total control over my impressionable and vulnerable life. This was my battle at 16, young, fresh and pretty.

He would karate chop and kick me, wear me down and weaken my ability to fight back. The psychological, physical, social and emotional degree that people on every level in life try to make you, compel you to be what they want and need you to be is alarming and widespread. Changing my identity by altering my nature was his constant pursuit and

I felt trapped and couldn't go back home. He would parade around the house, naked and erect trying to tease me and convert my will. His penis was very large. I was very pretty or handsome if you will and he was dangerously determined to break me like a horse you want to ride. As I started out 50 years ago, I'm still fighting to live and be who God created me to be and not who and what everybody else needs me to be. And it all started in church where ultimately my call and purpose would be and represent God, whom I am called to serve. The contrast just gets deeper and deeper. My journey has yet to result in what I want but what many in my circle needs me to be. I endured it because I convinced myself to believe that it was my duty to suffer for others, as Christ suffered for me.

Had I given in to this man's power, pressure, sick, perverted and ungodly nature and psychological manipulation of my vulnerability and need for him, I would have become a by-product of who he was. What he wanted and possibly never realized my destiny. The devil (opposer) steals, kills and destroys. The Devil thought he had me, my destiny, faith and death, but I got away. Greater is he that is in me (guiding my every footstep), than he that is in the world. He did not break me in, I broke away. Guide my feet Lord, Master, I know you can. Hold my hand Lord and lead me to the promised land. Be my friend Lord and keep me away from sin. Oh Lord, oh Lord, I know you can, I know you can. I still attest today that Jesus knew me long before I knew him (acknowledged, accepted). He had been with me all the time. He promised, lo, I will be with you. If you make your bed in hell, I will be there with you. I will never leave or forsake you. Holding on to, staying connected to anything or anybody that deeply, deteriorates and diminishes the quality and substance of your life and purpose is death. Living a life that is a false,

distorted or forced representation of who you are is death. Who you are or purposed to be dies. Who others are or encourage you to be, lives. God said to Jeremiah: I knew you before you entered your mother's womb. That's where I touched, assigned your destiny and started directing your path in spite of the stony road you traveled to get there. Never give in to and give up on who you are and what you are strongly inspired to be. There's a message in and a mission to the madness. Many of us are not living out the true meaning of "Who We Are". God's unique creation on assignment. Strangely enough, over the years, connection to the gay life being pressed against me, continued and seemed to confirm the purpose of my existence.

Sometimes in our pain and association we become products of our environment so much so that we begin to draw the conclusion that God made us this way. This is God's will for my life. The power of persuasion. In one of Dr. King's speeches he stated that, "if you tell somebody something, loud enough and long enough, they will eventually start to believe it". By association, influence and consistency, we start to slowly become molded into something we are not. Watch what you say and do all around your children in their vulnerable and impressionable years. And this misguided, Mis-channeled and Misdirected emotional rollercoaster began to develop a mind-set. At one point, all of my friends coincidentally or planned, were gay and sadly I eulogized all of them from the pandemic death of AIDS. Every single one of them. I was performing so many funerals and making hospital visits that I became labeled as an "AIDS preacher". My sensitivity, genuine compassion and moral support for them during this lonely, abandoned, embarrassing and debilitating death found me at their bedside sharing their final moments of hope in utter despair, with my purpose and identity, intact.

So yes, starting out at 16 when I left home, it seemed to be an honorable and simple pursuit. Finding my way, establishing my identity, my place in the universal order of things and showing my mother that all of her love and sacrifices were not in vain. To be better and to do better. All 10 of us lived in the same ghetto, same rat-infested one- bedroom house where heat and air conditioning were not a commodity, and with the same alcoholic father. She would constantly blame herself for our living conditions. My attempt was to show her that ultimately our fate was in the choices we made. We were all on the same playing field. Out of that family, some were gay, hustlers, robbers, preachers, pastors and liars. All of us, as we grew up and based on our learned behavior, DNA, or desired interest, made choices. As is the case in many of our children's lives, we mold, direct, feed, impart morals, ethics, disciplined and principled behavior, but when our children grow up and take responsibility for their own lives, they go where they want. They do what they want. They live the way they want. It's called freedom of choice. Their behavior when in charge of their own lives, doesn't always reflect what we expect. While we as parents can and should have a major influence in their lives, rebellion and peer pressure seems to dominate the path they choose. If one of her children could break the trend and find their way to a more acceptable and honorable lifestyle, then all of us had that same opportunity. All of the dynamics were identical. I did not want her to have to live with and bear all of the burden for how we lived. I chose out of love for her to show and prove to her that life can be better and I was going to be her living example. However, this pattern that my life would take, made that task extremely difficult.

I was told once by my Bishop to guard my heart. I wish I had listened. Being used, manipulated, putting others first, always blamed for others failures and exhausting all of my resources for others in return for their ungrateful, inconsiderate, insensitive and unappreciated accusations was my unwarranted and unwanted destination. This phenomenon was exacerbating and draining. Needless to say, I felt deeply the pain of my mother's sacrifices and unconditional love and I wanted to fix it. Even today at the age of 89 when she immerses herself in a refreshing and relaxing bubble bath, she wipes over the bruises and scars that my father inflicted on her for 49 years. Bathing in sweet-smelling fragrances and oils, like women do, every stroke of her washcloth reminded her of the constant pain she suffered. How do you forgive and forget what you have to look at every day of your life? There was a time at the age of 17, when I could not endure it any longer. I boldly informed my father that I had made a decision, that I was going to be gay and that if he put his hands on my mother to hurt her one more time, I was going to kill him, and serve the next 30 years of my life in prison. This was my foundation for being gay. Real talk. Because I was young, fresh meat and pretty and I knew what that reality looked like in prison. For my mother, I was willing to endure that end. This phenomenon has gripped my life. Giving all, I have so others may live as God desires. I guess it's in my heart, my DNA. It's who I am, what I am. Jesus said, "I came that you might have life and that more abundantly ". I died so you could live. This spirit seems to have embodied my life. I'm still learning that it was only necessary for him to die one time for humankind, and not me.

One day, I found my brother behind the couch, on top of my

brother, having sex. I never told my mother. I don't know if this experience at such a young age contributed to the gay life, he felt compelled or chose to live. Who will ever know the impact of such an action? Sex, an act or performance worthy of serious thought and evaluation. It can be an instrument of pain and physical gratification. It can be an expression of mutual care and admiration, or it can be a weapon of vengeance and control. In any case, it has the power to persuade and permanently influence life, nature and behavior especially when prematurely experienced at the wrong time, with the wrong people and the wrong way. I do know that sex out of order can cause disorder in defining how those feelings influence what you become.

Sex is the most powerful, sensational and stimulating attribute ultimately expressed in an orgasmic climax and once the body experiences it, it thrives for a repeat performance. Sex is a weapon and all too often used to maneuver and manipulate one's way in life. Many have achieved heightened levels of success because of who they have slept with. Sex has started wars, destroyed countries and families. I heard a pastor say once that "the problem with men is that they think with the wrong head". Truly, we need more preachers that will give it to you hard and from the pulpit and not participate in and camouflage its seriousness. He said that we think with the head below our waist and not the one above our neck. I believe that God's intent when he orchestrated our bodies in his own image was that sex would represent those instruments used to express one's love and commitment to another. It is why in early centuries, when you had sex with someone, you were permanently bound to them for life.

This concept is confirmed in Ruth 4:13. "So Boaz took Ruth. and

she became his wife: and he went in unto her. "Note the order, wife then sex. This concept is further established in 1 Corinthians 6:16, "Do you not know that he who unites himself with a prostitute is one with her in body". From a Biblical standpoint that "once you lay with her you stay with her". Sex may have been what changed the order and course of my brother's life.

Sex out of order can cause disorder. An attempt by a pastor to convert me or some other selfish use is an example. That explosion of sensation bonds lives, all of the dynamics connected to those lives. Your first love (sexual encounter, corrupter of your virginity) is the encounter that measures all that comes thereafter. You never forget your first love and all that follows often compares to it. Sex is powerful and extremely dangerous when used the wrong way. There was a debutante who entered in the room of a fighter late one night and took off all of her clothing, opened her legs and as the fighter prepared to penetrate her, she claimed her right to change her mind. Sex is not a toy. It can destroy and render devastating results when used as a weapon or controlling device. It destroys reputations, businesses and can impede our pursuit of quality living. He had sex with her and they became one. Sex bonds. It secures and glues. Entertain for a moment the Biblical reality that you're permanently connected to everyone you've laid with. *"Baby Mama Drama"* just went viral. When you inject my DNA into your body, it becomes a part of you. It enters into your life producing channel and produces a life that is symbolic of my nature and character. How many people are you spiritually and physically bonded to, connected to forever. Sex does not define, it combines.

One criteria often used in determining who we want to be with or live with forever is whether they're good in bed. For many, it's probably at the top of the list when searching for a mate. It becomes the determining factor in relationships. Sex does not make relationships successful. It is simply an expression of a feeling between two people which in time will fade or cease to function, resulting in an inability to perform, such as, atrophic vaginitis (dry, itching, irritating and pain), erectile dysfunction, and enlarged prostates. If the foundation of a relationship is built on sex, when sex dies so does the union. I urge you to consider the story of Mary and Joseph in Matthew 1:18. His mother Mary was pledged to be married to Joseph, but before they came together, she was found to be pregnant (by) the Holy Spirit. What was first and essential in this relationship surviving the absolute worst of circumstances, including they're unique and unified ability to support a child on a huge mission was Jesus. They had to First overcome the fact that the woman I'm engaged to marry is pregnant. You can do the math. Their union (to be married first), was built on his ability to protect and understand his wife's cause, condition. Their joint assignments to care for this child, purpose, value, substance and commitment to a mission. The institution of marriage reflects God's relationship with mankind and cannot be built on some temporary fleshly and emotional climax. So, can't your life. The adverse consequences of sex when taken out of order and context can affect content. It can result in or cause disruption in identifying and defining our perceived roles in life. Sexuality before intellectuality can lead to immorality and that changes the game. It can destroy natural and wholesome relationships. It causes confusion, conflict and misguided expectations. Today one of the determining criteria in marriages and relationships are based on how good you are in bed. That's the foundation. Not one's moral and ethical support in life. Emotional support in the loss of a loved one, a shoulder to cry on, compassion and commitment in dark times. And when those expectations are lacking, and not expressed, and there is no trust, it causes pain, void and emotional disappointment. In large, because that character was not a part of the deal or the priority. The foundation was built on the ability to satisfy a fleshly desire. It is a stress relief valve. An instrument or activity we turn to let off steam, such as "my baby had a bad day". That's the huge investment we make in the beginning of our affairs and you get what you pay for. And we are left alone and disappointed in our midnight hours. When sex becomes the dominating factor, fueling our lives, when it's over or when we are unable to perform, it is seriously challenged and dangerously impaired. Our fate is limited on our ability to perform.

When a child is raped, sexually violated, it can change or permanently alter their identity, especially when there is no therapeutic absolution. It has the potential of changing their natural normal and healthy interaction, involvement, roles in intercourse and relationships with their sex partners for a lifetime. Introducing a child to such a powerful entity can cause a shift in behavior, attitude, expectation, trust, isolation, loneliness, discomfort rebellion and revenge.

Subjecting a child to an act of sex or penetration before it's time when they are unprepared mentally, physically and unconditioned emotionally can cause deep psychological instability. Processing these acts to their bodies prematurely can result in damaging repercussions. An ongoing occurrence of events in this traumatic state can become a matter of life and death.

It can cause aggressive and controlling tendencies. A desire to have sex in positions that makes them the aggressor and to avoid the painful memories of their experience so as to not allow them to be repeated. Sex for them can become a weapon of revenge and not an expression of love and mutual admiration.

I share this profound and life-changing issue in which all too often goes unnoticed and undetectable only in context of me finding my identity and how that component at the age of 16 could have altered my direction and changed the course of my life and who would have ever known. All too often our lives are captivated and driven by that physical sensation and stimulus that controls our choices and decisions. Sex wrongfully applied could have changed my identity and pursuit forever.

Today in reflection, as I close out the first chapter of my life, I am reminded that God was guiding my feet, a light unto my path. that he had been there with me even though I had not accepted or acknowledged his existence as a keeper and sustainer. As a matter of fact, I hadn't been in a church since the age of seven or eight in a town in Snow Hill North Carolina.

At the age of 17, in search of a more disciplined life and environment I entered the United States military to put me back on Focus and obtain my high school diploma. Because of my immediate challenges, when I left home I was off track, on the wrong road, and life had taken a different turn. I was actually 17 when I enlisted and entered into adulthood. My military ID was the first document that legally considered me grown. Maybe I'm still a little bit ahead of my time. Maybe therein lies my challenges in life. Too advanced for my present to understand

and realize my intellect, insight and intent. During my tenure as a soldier, I visited 38 States and three countries. I drew and enjoyed many friendships and Associations. My prized possession was my orange book that I established which contained all of my wonderful contacts. Over the years because of my unstable and constantly moving path, I lost my orange book to my total disappointment. I received my GED and took several courses in Psychology in an attempt to learn how the human mind works. In part, I suppose because of my confusing beginning, the pattern my life had taken, human behavior, and a search for who I am as a teenager still on a mission, I needed to slow down, settle my mind, grasp my identity and decide what course life would take.

The United States military did provide for me a protected environment, so I thought. This protected environment, the United States military, took me to my last duty station in Bitburg Germany, just four hours south of Frankfurt in 1975 for eight months. Immediately upon my arrival in Bitburg, I engaged in confiscating 18 grams of 98 percent pure heroin. My daily intake of this drug was the equivalent of a $400 a day habit. When I departed the U.S. military in September 1975, my friends and associates cried and mourned for the fear that the wrong use of this drug in the United States would overtake me. However, when I arrived back in the U.S., I never touched the stuff again. While at the club one night I encountered an altercation with a young man. He was fully intoxicated and drugged, and I recommended that he leave the club and return to our barracks. Surprising to me he returned to our barracks, confiscated a large knife and returned to stab me on my left side, one-fourth of an inch from my heart. I believe it was the results of that stab wound that I carried Hepatitis C in my body for 44 years. I came to understand later that he had a history in the military of causing all kinds of disorderly conduct and they were seeking a source for his dishonorable discharge. In the military's pursuit to take him down, they strongly compelled me to press assault charges against him and testify on behalf of the military.

It was not my desire or intent to do so or to further harm his already destructive career. Because of a man's bad judgment and childish behavior, it was not in my heart or my spirit even to my pain and subsequent loss to cause another man harm. I understood his misfortunate behavior and sacrificially was not willing to cause him any further harm. Because I refused to participate in their endeavor and to be used to further someone else's agenda, the military dismissed me earlier than my release date with a discharge that was not favorable. It has haunted and adversely affected my career and benefits for 46 years.

So here once again I was unable to escape these phenomena of being forced to be and do what someone else expected and wanted. to use me for their own personal gain and cause me to suffer because I cared. I was blessed in 2018 to receive the miracle Hepatitis C cure. I have not fought bears like David or lions like Daniel, but I am unshaken and unwavering fighting and standing for what I believe is good and right. No matter what the cost. I'm not, or ever have been easily swayed, possibly to my detriment. I was told once that my life would be complex, technical and unorthodox. It has been on course to meet that prophetic word. I was also told that my greatest strength would be my weakness. And my heart has proven that to be true also. The basic, simple attributes of Christ, whom I'm sold out to are unconditional love, sacrifice, giving my all, looking beyond faults, and meeting people at their needs has in

reverse caused the greatest weakness and created avenues that people have used me abused me and attacked me. The internal battles that I have fought have often weakend me but the Apostle said that when I am weak, that's when I'm the strongest. Because that's when I totally rely on Christ to bring me through. I fought the Cadillac Corporation once who assured me that they were bigger, their forces were more vast, and that I would not win the battle. I simply responded, see you in court. A high school dropout mind you. I stood, unafraid, victorious and relentless on what I believed was a right and appropriate resolution. Before we were scheduled for court, I received a call from one of the many lawyers they claimed were equipped and always ready to fight their battles. He offered me everything. I had requested more than $1,000 and he delivered it to me within 24 hours. Holding on to what I believe has cost me in every situation in life to date. Money, reputation, credibility, and blame. In chapter nine of my life, church number three, years ago there was a cry for help, among the members there was a feeling of being used and not treated respectfully. They felt they were being violated and were unimportant. I stood for right then. I stood for an accurate application of God's word in his church. I stood and fought for what was in the best interest of all God's people. But when the battle got heated, things didn't turn out well. The powers to be were prevailing and intimidating. I was accused, abandoned and attacked. I became the problem because I stood and fought against the problem. At every turn in life, my good was turned into evil. there has been an interference in my cause. An interruption in my identity, character, reputation and integrity that left internal scars, while my labor and sacrifices seemed unproductive. Stand against wrong and be blamed for the wrong. Leaving for my mother, finding my identity for my life and establishing the military as a foundation has resulted in being a dropout, converted into homosexuality, going to jail and permanently labeled dishonorable or unfavorable.

What a complex contrast. At this point, at every turn, what I stood for and believed morally and ethically, was questioned, tested and turned into evil and a misrepresentation of my intent. The quality of the life I was promised by God and the desires of my heart at every turn have been threatened.

To this end and even as I approached 20 years old, I've had to consistently grapple with that question: Do I hold on and Die. Or Let Go and Live?

Do I hold on and be steadfast in my Pursuits?

Or

Let Go --- give it to God and keep it moving

Chapter 1

Sermonic Lesson

WITH A MADE-UP MIND
Philippians 2:5

I'm reminded of a story told by Dr. Martin Luther King, Jr. He said that one night as he sat at home, sipping a cup of coffee and thinking of the difficult journey ahead as they prepared to march for sanitation workers, he became overwhelmed. There had been threats on his life, to kill him and his family and threats to burn his house down, with all of them in it. He was totally immersed in his concern for his family and their safety. Was it fair to subject them to the tortuous danger and perils he faced in his pursuit for a better world? There was an even greater cause if one can conceive that. The mission for which he was called and gave his life for. As he sat there he entertained the thought that if a man has nothing for which he is willing to die for, then he is not fit to live. As I sat there, he said, in this deep trance, I heard the words of an old hymn. I've seen the lightning flashing. I've heard the thunder roar. I have felt sin breakers dashing. Trying to conquer my soul. But I heard the voice of Jesus, telling me still to fight on. He promised never to leave me. Never to leave me alone.

In Jeremiah 1:5 God said to him, before I formed you in your mother's womb, I knew you. It seems inevitable to glean from the story that God has put us all on a path to fulfill. As you journey into the unknown, the unsure and unpredictable, your pathway and passion for life will be unveiled. It's life processing. it will get turbulent and frightening at times. Don't panic. Just stay focused, and stay the course. There is something greater than any one of us at Play, working for the betterment of all of us. A cause or movement greater than you, working in you. After graduation from college and accepting the role as Pastor of Ebenezer Baptist Church in Atlanta, Georgia, Dr. King received a call from the Southern Christian Leadership Conference. The issue involved a young black woman named Rosa Parks who was arrested from sitting in the front seat of a bus where blacks were prohibited. He was called to assist them in the matter. This sparked one of the greatest moves in the world and changed his course and path forever. Changes, challenges and controversy will come. Sometimes we don't know when or how but we do know that they are revealed in life as we go. As they occur or begin to develop as in the life of Jeremiah, know that the spirit of Christ is at work performing his perfect will for your life and the greater cause that's within you. All things will work together for your good if you keep your mind stayed on him who is the author and finisher of our faith. he will give you peace. Let this mind be in you that was also in Christ Jesus who knew you before your mama conceived you.

In closing, be reminded that Jesus at the age of 33, hanging on a cross

at Calvary, in spite of the uncertainties of Life, the sacrifices and sufferings that one man made for all men, revealed that it wasn't about him. He said not my will but thy will be done. And with a made-up mine, in the words of Marvin Gaye who said "let's get it on", and he stayed the course. He swallowed his pride, ignored the enemies and bystanders, put his hands to the plow and never looked back. Thank God Almighty , he never looked back. He would not come down from the cross, to save himself. He hung there and died just to save me.

Chapter 2
First Relationship, First Born 1976

I n 1975, shortly after returning from my three-year tour in the military, I met my first born's mother. I admit that after being an adult / Soldier for three years, moving back home to Washington DC with my mother and family was not quite what I had anticipated. Life doesn't always look like you envisioned or planned and the path to its fulfillment is sometimes unexpectedly more rugged than you anticipated. However, the journey to reaching your desired goals, whether good, bad, or indifferent, can reward you a wealth of wisdom and knowledge. In this chapter of my life, the continued pattern of me losing at every turn became clearly evident. Going beyond the norm and expected, and taking

responsibilities for the actions of others continued to develop. However, I must admit that this chapter, even though it ended up ugly and painfully challenging, rewarded me with one of the greatest gifts that I could imagine.

Upon returning from duty, I met, moved in with, and started a relationship with my first child's mother. We lived together in a small efficiency apartment on 16th Street in Northwest Washington, D. C. Shortly thereafter she conceived a child. This child was my parents first grandchild who became spoiled by the entire 10-member family beyond what is imaginable. One day when I arrived home from work my then three-month-old daughter was lying in her bassinet while the entire apartment was totally consumed with smoke from marijuana. An innocent three-month-old infant inhaling this large quantity into her underdeveloped lungs, a drug that alters the mind. I was outraged. I informed her mother and her best friend that they had 30 seconds to clear the air or themselves from that room or be forcefully ejected by me. I smoked cigarettes at the time but never around my child. My daughter's name is Tanita Joy McLaurin, as it is recorded on her birth certificate, and I jointly cared for her. Our child grew while our shared living only lasted a short while after this incident. Her name was derived from the inspiration, feeling and need that I had at that juncture in my life. I needed "Joy". I wanted "Joy". To need a Joy was the aspiration in my heart. Ta-nita-joy was the name attached to that aspiration and that's what she brought me and my family for years to follow. One day, at the age of 11, I was served a notice from the court by her mother for child support and paternity. Someone was in her ear and the price we pay when we allow outside influences to manipulate our decisions, can be unbearably costly. While there were moments during our short-lived relationship that I sensed or perceived were unfaithful, it did not take root in my spirit because it was overwhelmed by my love for my bundle of joy. I simply ignored the subliminal indicators, which would soon result in an explosive and devastating reality. My love, responsibility and total devotion was now in question and I was introduced to the world as a deadbeat dad. All too often, too many black men get caught up in the grievous, vengeful and greed tactics of our baby mama drama and add to the stereotypical stigma attached by our society. That is not who I am or was created to be. I acknowledged that this was my child. I sincerely loved her madly and I will go to any extreme to care for her. Her mother's pursuit was an unsubstantiated evil act. I questioned her motives and intent and stated my concerns to her that this selfish and inconsiderate action instituted against me was without Merit or rationality or any compassionate concern for our child and was simply money driven. It was to manipulate me for money when all that was expected of me as a good father was in full operation in our lives since her birth. While foolishly denying my premise, I reminded her that in her action against me, paternity had already been established, leaving child support as the only agenda. By law I was informed that I had to take a blood test and it would cost me $300 to determine what I had already acknowledged and accepted and forced me to fight for something already established. Evil.

She continued her pursuit. The results of the blood test that I was compelled to take, based on scientific DNA, indicated that I couldn't possibly be the biological father of this child. I was not surprised, but deeply cut to the core of my being. In this process it was determined that

the father was of African descent and our child's mother had been in an affair with a foreign partner during our relationship. One day we were in heaven and the next day in hell. Unfortunately, that day when I was informed of the court's findings and conclusions in the case, and they're not so encouraging words to my baby mama, I was given the task of shattering my baby's life with this news. The risk of losing what totally filled my heart with joy for 11 years and the devastation it now brought to my family, our first grandchild and niece was too much to bear. The Bible says that God does not put more on us than we can bear, but on that day, I believe that he had lost track. My battles or challenges got worse as life progressed but this one, in the beginning of a 50-year journey was a task to reckon with. I was twenty-one years old. This assignment was a test of true genuine love, unconnected by the power of the blood, but of the spirit and will of man.

In the basement of my mother's home on Columbia Road in Washington D.C., I met with my eleven-year-old daughter and shared the results of the test her mother forced us to undertake. We immediately began to weep together and the tears seem to have never stopped. It is often (ironic) that those who wreak havoc on others conveniently escape the immediate and painful repercussions of their actions and inability to resolve them. I received my first sexually transmitted disease and dis-ease in this relationship and still have the marks to show it. Once again, I realized that even though I did not know God nor had I acknowledged or accepted him in my life, he had been there all the time, guiding my feet and ordering my steps. In adversity, I was tremendously blessed.

All that we knew or understood to be, in the newness of life and love was now threatened to be snatched away. What was I to do now? What was I to say now? How was I supposed to feel now? Where do we go from here was consuming all that we had come to know and accept? Like Christ who comes to salvage the damage done in and to our lives, to fix us, to repair and replenish all the suffering sacrifices that cause great loss is all at our feet.

As we sat there crying and wondering, how do we fix this broken reality and minimize this devastating blow to our spirit. We both had decisions to make, or did we? I was 33 years old and she was 11. We made two life-long decisions that day that could have changed our lives and the course of our destiny. I informed my daughter that as it ends up in most cases, at some point in life she will develop a desire to trace her roots, to know who her real father is or out of curiosity, a yearning connection within her to know her family. At the age of 11, she adamantly stated that I know who my real father is. You are my real father and I will never desire or need to search for anyone else. This was her decision. I added to that. that you are my daughter and additionally we decided that this is the way it is and we will never discuss the matter again. Others have attempted to pierce that bond, to discuss and engage or remind us of our reality, but were met with a painful and dangerous rebuke. Joy remains one of God's greatest gifts to me, I remain the father that she loves, accepts and defends like a mad Black woman if you test her. I have a beautiful, intelligent and loving granddaughter because of Takiiya and will soon enjoy my first great-grandchild. Oh my God, I'm old.

As I close out the second chapter of my life, it is clear that embedded deeply in my spirit and heart, at age 33, was a willingness to take responsibility and accountability of others' issues as my own. While in

many cases this has been painful but is now a character trait. Attacked, I was willing to sacrifice my life for others and care for their mistakes and bad judgments, even when they did me wrong. Romans 7:21 says that when I would do good, evil is always present. But Genesis 50:20 confirms that what man meant for evil, God meant it for good. This era of my life, this series of wrongs enacted against me was rewarded with something good. This one, unlike some that will soon follow, was easy. Love made it easy. In the seventies the Soul Children sang this song:" Love makes it right". God meant (converted) this one for good. For those attached to this era, being used and manipulated was a "Life filled with Joy" Go Figure! This deadbeat daddy image, lifetime role as a father, this disease, resulted in a Life filled with JOY" In this situation I can sincerely assert that: if Jesus was willing to die for me, then I am willing to live for him, and for her. A doctrine and a choice that has rewarded me and enhanced the quality of my life for 44 years.

The Bible says that the enemy, like a thief in the night, comes at unawares, to steal, kill and destroy. He came that day to steal my joy. That day my precious Joy and I did not choose to hold onto disappointment, emotional pain, embarrassment, humiliation, and Hate. These are all attributes that diminish the quality of life God desires and causes some elements of death and deterioration. We chose life and that more abundantly. We let it go and let God. Literally gave it over to him and forgot it ever existed.

I believe as you encounter similar challenges in your life, if you were to apply my life and lessons, consider the ultimate plan God has for you as he promised in Jeremiah 29:11," I know the plans that I have for you, they are good and not evil to bring you to an expected end. And trust that all things will work together for your good". That you too will know when and how to:

HOLD ON AND DIE OR LET GO AND LIVE

Chapter 2

Sermonic Lesson

WHEN I WOULD DO GOOD
Romans 7:21

W hen I think of the humanitarian dynamics we experience, it often astonishes me in the context of Creation. God created us in His image and likeness. He provided a perfect habitation for us to dwell in the Garden of Eden. He gave us perfect health, authority, dominion and even a long life. What did we do in response? We rebelled, disobeyed, rejected and even forgot he existed. No loyalty, gratitude or sense of duty to do right by him. We literally destroyed any decent or respectable ability to even come into His presence or more over engage in any conversation with him as we were able to at some point. But he didn't give up on us. he developed another source to restore our broken relationship with him by allowing his only son to die to redeem us back into good standing, and what did we do? We rejected Christ and crucified him. But he didn't stop there. He sent his spirit to hang out with us and help guide and direct our paths on Earth until he decided to rejoin us. We rejected God our creator, killed his son, our Savior and quenched his spirit, our guide. It all doesn't seem to make sense sometimes but in creation we were all given free will and choice. It's how we are made. There are always two spirits at work in us. Warring constantly, if you will. God's spirit and man's. Right and wrong. Good and evil. We always have the choice to pick the one we believe best benefits our motives and agendas. We are a most rebellious, untoward and ungrateful people. I believe that's why the first words that Jesus spoke before he died for us were "Father forgive them for they know not what they're doing".

Sometimes fear, greed, outside interferences and what others think, influences our behavior as we wrestle against flesh, blood and spiritual wickedness in high places and it causes us to do some crazy stuff. Sometimes when we should be exhibiting Eternal gratitude, for the role others play in our lives, we are led to adverse actions. After observing all of the good works Jesus did, including healing his own mother, Peter acted like he didn't even know Jesus. For the good that I would do, evil is always present. As long as Satan reigns so does the evil spirits that have rallied to his cause. Sometimes your good deeds are twisted and made to look evil based on the intent and motives of others. But Jesus said, Father forgive them for they have no idea what they do or how they have been used. Luke 6:27-28 says "love your enemies, do good to them which hate you. Bless them that curse you and pray for them which despitefully use you". Out of all the good that I've done and been, how could you just stab me in the back like that? But even while we were yet sinners and coming short Christ died for all. Practice and learn how to look beyond faults and see other's needs. Bear one another's burdens. That's what he did for us and one day that recompense is going to be required of us. Every good and perfect gift comes from God (my daughter Joy). Look for God in all things and in all people. He said, I am all, I am in all, I am through all, and I am above all. No situation escapes him. He uses whom he will, when he will, where he will, and how he will. Forgive the evil or bad and in all that you do, do it to the glory of God. We were all created in His image and in his likeness. Choose ye this day good or evil.

Chapter 3

Marriage #1 & #2
1978-1979

I met my first wife in 1978-79, approximately one year after my military career ended. I was the assistant manager of a Peoples Drug Store, now CVS. I was young, energetic and free from the dominating control of the United States Air Force. My military experience had a lifetime effect on me. I decided at a very young age after taking orders for 24 hours a day and not having any real control of my own, that I wasn't taking orders anymore. This explains why I started my life being in charge. This four -year experience was the only job that I had in life working for someone else. The rest of my life to date, I have been an entrepreneur (self-employed). Even then in my life I began to experience

jealousy, envy and self-preservation from my superiors because of the quality of my work and the popularity that I was gaining with this predominantly white owned and operated family operation. One of my superiors, a district manager, was in his position only because the company was publicly forced to employ an absolute minimum percentage of African Americans to satisfy EEOC guidelines. As he saw me rapidly progressing and rising up in rank and potential advancement, he became threatened by my race, skill and energy. It was determined that he was afraid that I would benefit from the same resource he enjoyed and would ultimately replace him, so he created a situation to have me terminated. Admittedly, I was young, I was good. I was enjoying it and people had their eyes on me. My first private-sector job, I was attacked and targeted for being good and doing good, and jealousy and envy at the age of 21 became a part of the DNA that ignited my opposers for Life.

As the assistant manager of the Peoples Drug Store located at North Capitol and H Street Northeast in Washington D. C., I would often be seen in my upper level booth as you entered and exited the store. One day I looked down and noticed a short, attractive young lady staring up at me with a glare in her eyes, as she exited the store. This became a regular occurrence and eventually we met, dated and married. There was an occasion when we were making love that she began to tremble perversely, she was shaking, and her body was jerking. For a brief moment my ego arose and I became excited at my ability to perform, but I became increasingly alarmed at her behavior. I was not packed with that kind of machinery. There was no serious or detailed explanation offered and life continued. I went to work, gave her my paycheck and a six pack of Miller High Life and a pack of Kool cigarettes were my weekly allowance until the day she conceived our first child. The same day when my first wife announced her conception to me, she said, "I don't need you anymore". I was stunned at this statement. Personalities changed. Directions changed. Interests changed. It was as if her conception released her desire or need for me, and I became deeply troubled. Confused. I insistently pursued an understanding regarding this sudden shift in our relationship. One day while sitting on the front porch at her mother's drinking beer she revealed to me that her daughter had been raped years before we met, got pregnant from that rape, fell down the stairs and lost the child. Oh, my God. All of the lights went on in my mind. When we were having sex that day, it was in the exact position that she was raped and the symptoms were identical to the trauma she experienced. There was a deep void from the loss of her child and there was no therapeutic treatment from the trauma she experienced. In her psyche, when she conceived our child, the long-awaited void had been filled. It was as if she had subconsciously used me and now had no need of me. I'm reminded of the United Negro College Fund theme, "the mind is a terrible thing to waste". Therapy is such a vital instrument after any traumatic experience in helping to restore rationale and reason to healthy relationships. So, there I was, early in my life, suffering the consequences, and paying the price for the damage someone else caused or experienced not knowing all of the Demons I was fighting against. Decades later as a pastor there was a theme attached at the end of all of my communications in an attempt to exemplify as Christ did when he took all of our issues and suffering upon himself. It stated, ``Please forgive me for all of the wrong that others have caused in your life. I sincerely apologize". The significance of this situation in contrast is astonishing. There I was, at the age of 21 trying to bring resolve, survival, sustainability, and commitment to a cause and vow to such a huge emotional and psychological dilemma, as a high school dropout. We lived together for one year after she conceived and were married for four years on paper. With this hidden, unaddressed Monster daily lurking, our relationship was challenging and she asked me to leave.

Later she asked to return acknowledging her contributions to its failures. She had the baby. The void was filled but the effects of the psychological trauma were never addressed. Not realizing the real depths of our issues which often were wrongfully applied, she took the regular route using the court to attack me and subject me to the typical and Infamous deadbeat daddy drama. Because of a legal mix up in the ongoing transfer of our case to other jurisdictions in her attempt to track me down and take me for everything she could. Support doubled and reached up to $65,000 in arrearages.

I did not have the financial capacity to fight City Hall and tried to live a reasonably comfortable life. Child support was being illegally demanded from two jurisdictions and she refused to correct the issue. Subsequently, most of my tax returns, with my third wife years later were garnished. My passport was suspended and travels were limited to the United States only. After a 20-year tour in the United States Army and 40 years later, the child that she conceived and filled the void from her rape experience, demanded that she rectify the matters that she knew were wrongfully applied to her father. In reflection, I remember the applause in court from my first wife's family on an occasion when I was handcuffed and escorted from the courtroom.

I'm reminded of a cliche in life that embodies the theme of this book, and that is;" choose your battles". There comes a time in life when our battles are paramount. When we have to choose between two evils. It is clear that we can't fight everything all the time. It steals from our time to live, to be free, happy and enjoy all of the beauty that encompasses us. We can't fight it all. All is not ours to fight. There is a time and a season for everything under the sun. It was not my season nor in my best interest at the age of 21, trying to establish a foundation, to engage in such a monstrous task. We don't know who to fight or what hidden issues we are really fighting. Sometimes we have to make conscientious choices and decisions whether or not to hold onto issues and philosophy that are consuming. Mountains that are too high to climb. Waters that are too deep to swim. Battles that are too hard to fight. Life sometimes can be as simple as choosing whether to go or stay. Whether to lay down or get up, or as complex as holding on to things or people that are draining our aspirations and restricting our livelihood. Depleting our resources, diminishing us in value and substance and diminishing the quality of Our Lives. I found myself fighting against my wife's trauma, pain and void.

Do I hold on and die or let go and live?

Do I hold on to this bomb and fight or do I let go and let God?

Do I hold on to what is literally Killing Me Softly and Slowly, or do I let it go so that I can be free and live?

I chose to let go and live, and one of my greatest joys in life today, is that child that filled my wife's void.

It had to be between 1983 and 1984 that my relationship with my second wife began. I actually prayed one day for a young, pretty, godly,

talented mate who could play the piano. That description is what I thought I wanted and needed in a mate as a young Christian man. The perfect description of my desire. She was all of the above. I suppose we should be extremely careful about what we pray for because sometimes, for reasons of his own, God gives us exactly what we asked for. Little did I know that she would literally represent the most profound image and description of Satan himself. She was ten years younger than I was and of course there was no convincing me that age didn't make a difference. Oh, and how... She was the prettiest, petite and most precious gem you could imagine. She had a voice of silk and could sing your heart happy. She was a songstress, a piano player, and could quote scripture from Genesis to Revelation down to the commas and periods without even opening the book. She was 19 years old. What an exact response to my prayer to God. Even at that young age, she was so pretty and gifted that a renowned gospel artist who is now deceased featured her silk voice and face on an album with her performing his cover song. She was the epitome of talent and beauty. She was introduced into my very small inner circle by my deceased brother Michael early into the establishment of my third business. Joyful Star Child Development Center in Washington DC, in 1983. She and my brother were young and foolish. I would send them on errands in my cab only to find out later that they had been illegally working and charging cab fares. We became connected at the hip before marriage. Could not stay away from each other. I would often refer to her and I as Beauty and the Beast. This interaction didn't go well with her mother who became my biggest opponent, maybe because of my faith and my age. She began to attend church with me and sometimes supervised my two children while I worked or served in the pulpit. She really wasn't that much older than they were. One Sunday morning my son was not behaving properly. She reached her arm around the back of his neck and grasped his right ear and proceeded to twist it off of his head.

The members on the pew behind her became seriously alarmed at her action. They weren't aware at that time of her position in my life and what authorized this young lady to twist my son's ear off of his head. they reported her actions to me after service. Their concern didn't seem to bother her nor I. He behaved quite well after this incident and decided to respect her role in his life thereafter. Outside of church and in connection with my daycare center where she spent most of her time, we started a gospel group which included my brother and one of the parents enrolled. This was a very inspirational little group and we would periodically perform at churches and other events. The parent in the group began to draw close to me and I to her. As a young, Christian, single businessman, I made it clear to all frequently that I was not available to engage in any kind of relationship. I only had time to focus on my many activities at church and trying to build my daycare that was totally consuming. However, 0n the side, as a professional, with no expectations, I found a moment on occasion to get away. Ignoring my position not to enter into or commit to any relationship because of my schedule, the two of them and several others began to plot my movement and activity.

Over 85 percent of my parents were single mothers. My wife and the parent member of our group even set me up one night to prove that I was in an affair with both of them. Competition and possession became very dangerous enemies of mine. Many young ladies pulled at me simultaneously. Just a young up and rising entrepreneur trying to have a

little fun every now and then had become an outright battle. Right here, I'm reminded of Luke 8:17 which says "all things done in darkness shall come to light". The parent in our little gospel group became pregnant by me, of course. The baby was hidden behind her tubes unknowingly and almost killed her. The child did not survive. An innocent encounter by a consenting young man and woman one night just having some fun, was now a dead child and almost dead woman. Boy, life can flip the switch quickly. An innocent, hardworking attempt to build a dream had now become ugly and painful even though the daycare was growing tremendously. Somewhere in this process of time I had become a licensed preacher. Somewhere around 1984 or 1985 and I should have known better. Remember that I was sold out on Christ and his Doctrine. As a man, I slipped and I'm sorry, so sorry. I had become an example. Preaching God's will and his way in pulpits on Sunday morning while my flesh was rising up on Friday night. From the very moment, the very first time I learned about the cross, I fell in love with Christ, the cross and the need for my character and conduct to reflect the same. That's what should happen when you believe something and believe in something, your deeds should reflect. I don't play with God.

My second wife at that time also expressed a desire or called to be an evangelist. There was an occasion when she needed to prove that she was anointed and a gifted prophet. She was asked to speak at a revival service one week. While ministering, she called up a young man and informed him that a financial blessing was on the way to him. God told her. During the week she had the young man tracked down and given an envelope with money. During the final night of the revival, she called him back up to testify of how God had blessed him and to confirm the anointed power of her life to prove she was a prophet. It does not pay to play with God. If God has laid his gifted hands on you, all will know. You do not have to perpetrate a fraud. That behavior is of the devil. He is a deceiver of the people. The father of lies.

A minister of my staff one night, fell out on the floor. We call that being "slain in the spirit". A prophet had laid her hands on her and she laid out on the floor symbolizing her anointed power and Gods pouring into her life. A member went to aid her as she lay there. But she demanded for her to get away from me. She said I'm not out, I just want to make it look like it. Competition and a desire for power and prestige is corrupting the image of Christ and the effectiveness of his churches to change a generation. Let your light shine so that men may see your good works and glorify God. If it's in you, it will come out. Live the God that's in you and you won't have to perpetuate him out of you. My wife and I grew closer, yet not married, the daycare grew larger. It was now valued at $1.2 million. It was built from a raided whore house on Georgia Avenue in Washington D. C. to an honorable thriving institution by a high school dropout. I was truly on my way to fulfilling my vision to my mother and carrying out the mission she said I lived for, and I was only 33 years old. I was now in a territory that I had never experienced or expected. Single women were coming at me, making all types of offers. They were staff members and parents. I was in a world wind. "Take me and my family." "I'll be your slave", "You talk to other parents more than me." They were cornering and grabbing at me in the hallways. Waiting for me when the school closed. Then there came the ultimate threat. "If I can't have you, nobody else will." Out of all due respect, I was not brutal or arrogant in my constant rejections. I was just insistent

and committed to stay on my tasks and not mislead anyone. I have been told for years that if you have a weak marriage, do not go into business. If you have a weak business do not get married. I truly can understand the dynamics, the time-consuming energy that both require. And then one day on April 8, 1988 there was a report on the news station that said, "breaking news, "A preacher in a daycare on Georgia Avenue abuses children, story at 4:00"".

I will share more on this development in Chapter 6.

My life was immediately devastated. I was shattered. I was now seemingly immersed in A storm of rage, and rejection. A news reporter from Channel 9 had infiltrated my center and took inconspicuous videos to corroborate their headline. He was immediately relocated to another location. Because of media pressure, the city immediately ordered my Center to cease and desist. A dream destroyed at the mere snap of a finger. I believed the city violated 13 ordinances and subsequently I sued them for $36 million. I spent $100,000,00 on lawyers, trying to restore my name, credibility and dream. I was informed that this would haunt me for the rest of my life and that I should refrain from ever being around children. Where was my God? I was on trial for eight days. I was alone. I had no friends. I was publicly humiliated, could not work, and could not sleep. Disguised when I was in public. Resources drained. Image destroyed. All of my clients abandoned me. My blood pressure was in the strike zone. My church for 20 years turned on me and removed me from every level of leadership, and never once asked me if I was guilty or needed help. They called me the devil during worship. I had nothing.

I had no one. I was totally slandered.

When my wife found out that I was all alone and was suing for 36 million dollars she then wanted to marry me. Inside my heart I knew she only wanted me now because of the possibility of money. But I had no one else. I had nowhere to go. I was at my lowest. I married her because she led me to believe that I was innocent and she trusted me. I thought that maybe she was setting me up for revenge for the relationship with the other parent who lost my baby. Even though I was never in a committed relationship with anyone, I was traumatized. I didn't care. I needed somebody to believe in me and she was the only one in sight. How low do you go when you are at the bottom? On a technicality, I lost the lawsuit against the city of Washington, D.C. because I was one day late informing them of my intent to bring action against them. It was all over now. My life was over. My church deserted me and the world as I knew it was simply left to believe it was true. As soon as she found out that I had lost the battle, I served no more purpose for her, she immediately started her dismount. We had an apartment in Alexandria, Virginia. I was alone most nights, expecting that somebody would show up at some point. This was the only hope that I had so I tried to hold on to it. One night she came home late in the night and informed me that I was no longer capable of satisfying her sexually. She said I don't feel you. that I was more of a brother to her and not a lover. As I had suspected she had been with a Mandingo warrior with a pipe for an organ or a horse. Her vagina was wide open, when she spoke those words to me. I can't feel you anymore. Humiliate, demean and reject. I literally smelled the man. I couldn't perform and even if I could it was as if I wasn't even there. Physically or mentally. How low could I go trying to hold on to

all I had left? I tried to please her by performing oral sex while I smelled and tasted another man. Whatever I had to do to make her want me and stay with me. I cried and I cried, all night long.

Early in the morning, it must have been around three or four. I woke up, turned over, and looked Satan in his face. My wife---I saw Satan. He looked like E.T. in the movie years ago. He had several colors in his face which was dark and muscular. I don't believe that I was alarmed or afraid that morning, maybe it's because I was expecting him. I'm sure she did not perceive herself looking that way as she laid there. It was not her I suppose but I that had been a target of his deception and determination to destroy the Christ I live for. As Christ had become so real to me, immediately upon my knowledge of him, that night Satan also became real to me. That pretty, young, melodious, gifted and talented girl I prayed for and married was the Devil INCARNATE.

Unorthodox, technical, complex and REAL serious about the life and work that I do for God through Jesus Christ.

Our marriage lasted for three months holding on to what was killing, crushing and stealing all of my joy. Depleting all of my resources. Hold on and die, or let go and live. I let go and gave what I could not handle to God. I almost waited too late. "In all things give thanks and seek ye first the kingdom of heaven." In other words, measure everything against his word before you act on it. Don't quench the Holy Spirit that's constantly within you acting on your behalf. Remember, like The Prodigal Son, you don't have to ever stoop that low. God, your father is always waiting with open arms to receive you back home again and raise you up to that place he created you to be. More than a conqueror.

HOLD ON AND DIE OR LET GO AND LIVE

Chapter 3

AN ENCOUNTER WITH SATAN
Matthews 5:43-44

One day Jesus was having a conversation with Peter who was not only an Apostle but was also a man of sincere faith that Jesus knew God had authorized to help build the church. Jesus was explaining to his disciples that the time for him to die on the cross and return to heaven was drawing close. In opposition to his master leaving Earth and the great ministry that he had established, Peter responded, "O be it far from thee Lord." Jesus looking at Peter said "Satan I rebuke you. Get thee behind me." This powerful and anointed man of God for just a brief moment was overtaken by Satan in opposition to the will of God on Earth. Jesus was immediately able to discern that the spirit that was operating in Peter for that moment was Satan, more popularly known as the devil. He spoke to that spirit, not Peter. and he addressed him by name.

There are still Angels of Darkness or agents of Satan that are still operating in people in ways that we would never expect. It is healthy that we do not judge what we don't know and can't see. When these Spirits are in operation, we often confuse them with the body they inhabit. Jesus simply acknowledged and rebuked that demonic spirit and allowed Peter to complete his mission. He would build the church and the gates of hell would never be able to destroy it. It has been fully active for 2021 years to date. Satan still uses the weak, vulnerable, infirmities of others to destroy the work and will of Christ in you. John 10:10 says that Satan, like a thief, comes at unawares, in the night. A roaring lion seeking whom he may devour using whomever will allow him to catch you off-guard, when you least expect it, to kill, steal and destroy your dreams, your joy and your peace. He disguises himself as an angel of light. A wolf in sheep's clothing. Consider this, all that glitters ain't gold. Every closed eye ain't sleep. Every goodbye ain't gone. Peter's behavior was not a reflection of his title or mission in ministry. Sleeping with the enemy, living with, eating with or working with the Enemy often only attest to the spirit within those whom you care for or are close to and what's dominating their oppositional Behavior. Remember the Exorcist?

Yes, thou shalt love thy neighbour, but loving those who love you requires absolutely no effort. That's the easy way out. That's the microwave, quick fix approach. But what exemplifies the true nature of your love for Christ and desire to please God by fulfilling the real work of Christ on Earth is when you have mastered loving your enemies, blessing them that curse you, doing good to them that hate you and praying for them which despitefully use you and persecute you. The truth is that that seems to be The Road Less Traveled by on this Christian journey. But that's the cross that saved us. and so it behooves us to understand why Jesus taught this. That ye may be children of your father (God) which is in heaven: for He maketh his sun to rise on the evil and on the good, and sendeth rain on the just and on the unjust.

Chapter 4

Marriage #3
1982-2018

believe that I met my third wife at the first church that I attended. Ultimately, I gave my life to Christ there and many works over a 20-year period. Our real involvement however started when she enrolled her oldest daughter in the Child Development Center that I owned. Joyful Star Child Development Center. She wasn't very popular there at our church. As a matter of fact, she wasn't very well-esteemed because she was a struggling mother of four children by two fathers, although her three younger children were by her husband at the time. Their relationship was rapidly destructing because of his addictive vices. Unfortunately, my experiences in the Baptist Church including this one did not reflect a warm, graceful, compassionate and caring embrace for "sinful little girls". That's how she was looked upon and treated. However, the stigma attached to her name and reputation was clearly unfounded, unfair and inappropriate for any organization representing Jesus the Christ. A young, intelligent, hardworking, Christian preacher, business owner and DC cabbie, she grew to genuinely love and admire me.

My father, who died in 2000 of colon cancer along with many members and family, did not think that she was good enough for me. My mother's only disappointment was that I didn't inform her or my family of my intent to marry her until almost the day we were married in our church. My mother was very hurt, only because we shared everything with each other. I vowed never to keep my mother out of my loop. As you can imagine, I am a mother's boy. However, we began to develop a very cohesive and inspirational friendship. Sometimes I would walk to her house which was an hour's journey, just to be around her. I was very connected or sensitive to her challenges, struggles and dreams and I was also overcoming one of the greatest challenges of my life. She would often seek my advice regarding her unhappy, painful and seriously broken marriage. I was a fully licensed minister at this time in our church. I would encourage her to stay, forgive, pray and try harder, none of which were working for her. Of course, it seemed only appropriate to advise people on this regard without considering the depths of their issues. My point to her was that when and if she chose to walk away, after doing all she felt she could do, that her conscience would be clear, and that God would understand her heart and desire to please him in his Institution (marriage). When her marriage ended, I would walk that hour to see her

as we grew closer and more involved in each other's life and affairs. We were absolutely wonderful friends. I would visit her just to watch her kids so she could go out and be with friends, or have a drink. I cared for her children, taught them, guided them, helped them, loved and supported them. They were off the chain, did not respect her, or obey her and most of the time, just blatantly disregarded and ignored her right up through adulthood. They were at that time five, six, seven and nine years of age. Her home was in total disarray and out of her control. In frustration and deep concern for her sanity, one day I took her to an Econo Lodge and registered her to stay there for one week as a plan to personally correct the corruption in her home. She agreed. I went back to her home to receive the children from school and informed them that their mother could not handle things anymore. She was gone and would not be back. They all called my bluff and continued to argue and scream at each other, not doing their chores or cleaning up behind themselves. Expecting that this outside man was joking until the third day she didn't show up or speak to them. Unorthodox, technical and complex, remember? On the fourth day, the house was clean, chores were chartered and completed, conversations were respectful and all sibling issues and conflicts were discussed and agreed upon without outside involvement. However, I made sure that the mothers retreat lasted the entire week and miraculously she showed up and was graciously welcomed after seven days. Needless to say, they began to develop a sense of great respect for who I was, or more so, who I wasn't. Don't come for me, I'm not the one. Evidently, I had already begun a mission and she had no problems with it. In the absence of his father, her son was led to believe that at the age of five that he was the man now. What an awful developmental weight to bestow upon a child, long before they are mentally physically, financially or socially able to assume the magnitude of such a role.

Often it seemed appropriate to say in the absence of the father to appease the moment. Words are powerful even when used and taken out of context. They forced an intellectual, unintended pressure on him to perform and placed him in an impossible role. Eventually it became damaging to his character and position as a child. There is a process to developing a child into a man that extends far beyond mere words, but an untrained child in their vulnerable and ignorant state, tries to fulfill the mandate. My greatest role and challenge as a father to my wife's four children were with her son at that time.

One day in anger at his mother, he physically bucked up against her, full body in a totally unacceptable and disrespectful way. Without much thought I found myself pressing him up in the air, off of his feet, against the wall. Imagine that. He did what he felt was appropriate, via his training and mimicking his biological father's behavior, in the presence of the entire family. Out of all fairness to him, I had to back down on my approach. Because of his training and a heart murmur, I was limited in my reaction, Sensitive to all of the factors involved. So, I let him down off the wall gently, and apologized to him for my behavior and made a deal with him. Son, you were here first and you were told that you were the man. So, here's the deal. You can treat your mother any kind of way that you want to. You can do anything you want to your mother and you can disrespect her any time you wish because you were here before I was. However, you can never disrespect my wife or buck on my woman. You figure out how to disrespect your mother but respect my wife and we are good to go. Sleeping with his mother at the age of four, five and six is not a good healthy message to send to a young black man as we are experiencing in our Black culture today. It sends a false signal as we constantly hear about the devastating realities facing our young men. Her son had to learn that sleeping with his mother was transitional in preparation not permanent in lifestyle. He felt that the only man sleeping with his mother should be his father and as seemingly appropriate as it may seem and in fact deemed by God in his perfect family setting, it is not a present-day norm, but a five-year-old is not equipped to establish that parameter of understanding. Her son fought to maintain his stand and his mother fought to justify and tolerate his continuance.

A mother's love is precious, protective, binding and godly and never to be belittled or deprived, but it can often tolerate a behavior that can cause reversible damage. The mother needed to understand that she's preparing a son to be a man, father, husband and possibly provider. A son needs to understand that a mother chooses who she sleeps with, and I needed for her son to understand that nobody else sleeps with his woman, with any serious degree of regularity. When do we begin this process that in its season establishes a healthy balance? As a friend to my wife and even early into our marriage, I faced these profound challenges often with unorthodox methods. Uneducated, irresponsible, and unaccountability are overwhelming character traits that are plaguing the young population resulting in child support, baby daddy drama, jail and unemployment.

My wife's oldest daughter was often devastated in the early years of our marriage because of the participation she desired from her father until I assured her in his absence that I would always be there for her. I learned when she would come and sit on my lap and wrap her arms around my neck that I was in trouble. All of her four children growing up had to share their needs, experiences, and accomplishments with their fathers so that they could never blame my wife for their noninvolvement or negligence. But it was always clear that where they failed, I prevailed and they never missed a beat. Once, I went to the extreme of what a Godly (preacher) would engage. In my determination that her son's father would participate in at least one event in his life from birth through his first college graduation I offered to pay for two nights in a hotel where he graduated from, Pittsburg State, round-trip airline tickets and provide him with enough drugs for two days. What an offer and a determination? They thought I was crazy, but I was very serious and prepared to make the financial sacrifice. It didn't happen.

My wife's youngest daughter desired to be an actress from the age of four and we ensured that in her path forward, every move we made was to strategically connect her to the fulfillment of that dream. My wife and her children were unappreciated and disrespected by not only church, but family who were willing to see her and her children put out on the streets for the sake of possessing their inheritance (the family home).I recall while early in our relationship taking the position with our church and her family that, " while I don't know why you don't like or respect them, she's my wife now, they're my children now, the buck stops here now and I am a force to reckon with. I've been prepared for such a time as this. When you come for them, you are going to have to deal with me. Bold, right? On assignment. While my unorthodox, complex and Technical approach has continued successfully, it began to Intrigue my wife. Call it wisdom if you must. It worked and she had great respect for who I was and what we were accomplishing. She had great respect for who I was and as hard as she thought it would be after her husband, she was clinging to my every word. I was building a business. Joyful Star Child Development Center, a chain of five centers in the metropolitan area. I was also involved in many ministries in the church. I was sold out on Christ and his love for me. I had given my life to him and for him in 1980 after my first marriage failed and over a period of 10 years, I rarely missed a church service. But we found the opportunity to talk and hang out. However, even though she admitted to me that it may be difficult to submit to me, I should have listened to her. I was an entrepreneur and a preacher to the very core of my being, and I knew who I was and what I was. I was also compassionate and understood her circumstances and committing to her and her family was absolutely no issue for me. An associate minister and friend of mine at the time was preparing the thesis for her Masters or doctorate degree. Her subject was "children of alcoholic parents". Her paper was actually centered around me and the task that I had accepted when I married my wife. The direct symptom, she Associated to me in her Thesis was the sincere desire to prove or make something experienced better. My parents had eight children and my wife, and I together had seven. I was determined to prove to myself and my mother that life could be better than it had been for us. I was shocked at her studies and assessment. She loved teaching. It lends to why I was so determined to make it happen in spite of the cost, suffering, the sacrifices and ultimate failures. I wanted to fix my family, everything that my alcoholic father broke in his, and show my mother that her unyielding love was not in vain.

My wife shared that in her many challenges in life and painful marriage that she wrote God a letter. The letter read," please send me somebody that loves me, my children and God as much as I do" I cannot recall the number of times in open public church testimonies that she had testimony that I was the answer to her prayer to God. That was huge. I did not dispute her sincere belief that I was her answer and gift from Heaven. Maybe that letter should have been "returned to sender, for all it was worth. I did profoundly conclude that if God sent me to her, then I was on a mission from heaven and by any means necessary I would not fail. Angels never retreated nor were ever defeated. I accepted the mission. Unorthodox, technical and complex mission from God and so it was. God is still dispatching angels. This mission assignment is the mindset and attitude that I embodied for the entire 25 years of marriage to her. But somewhere on the journey she rejected me, my mission work (complex, technical and unorthodox) and subsequently the purpose God sent me to accomplish. Words are powerful. We should mind what we say and Proclaim. One day you will have to face it. Oftentimes in dispute or some disagreement, I would remind her of her request from God and my mission assignment to make her life work. It became my life's work. She would get offended and claim that I didn't love or care for her and her family and that she was "just a mission". I assert to you however; you want to spend it that greater love has no man than being on a mission from and for God himself. So often it was flipped from spiritual to flesh, when she did not like or agree with the process God used to bless us. God said, in all things, give thanks. I looked for God everywhere, all the time. When our way is priority, what we want, how we want it, and when we want it does not Prevail, we forget why we ask God or even that we ask God. He only asks that we trust him. His ways are not our ways and all too often I was accused of just doing me when there was no evidence that I gained from that. We acknowledge, pick and choose God's

assistance only when it supports our persistence. There was always someone gaining from what I was giving. I was told that I just wanted to do things my way and that I was using God to sell it. As a matter of fact, during my 15-year tenure as a pastor, I developed a pattern and conviction. I was labeled that everything I get I give away. Unlike many pastors people stopped giving me resources because they knew I would simply give them away. I could never be disappointed in that because God loved me so much that he gave me everything he had. These Godly character traits that I possess went unnoticed and rejected unless someone was on the receiving end. And so, fifty years has concluded that I ended up losing all while everyone in my path gained my all. One day I was left in the ditch bleeding to death and no one came to my rescue.

One day I received a revelation and I understood then why our life was so off the course God had planned when he answered my wife's prayer. She said," I don't hear you anymore". Words are powerful and we should be ever so careful when and what we speak. If you can't hear me, then you can't hear who sent me. If you reject me, then you reject who you said sent me. The course of our fate began to change. When you ask God for help, you don't reject his source because you don't like it or want it. I suppose that my purpose was no longer necessary and at that point I began to fight a losing battle. But as I accepted the assignment from God, I did not concede that God changed his mind, he just gave my wife and her family another chance like he always does. I sucked it up and stayed to task until I felt compelled to let go. It was draining me, depleting and deteriorating the quality of life that God promised and in turn making what seemed to be, useless energy and of no effect.

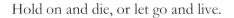

Hold on and die, or let go and live.

Die in purpose, substance, value, ethics, integrity and spirit?

In my first marriage of one year my wife said to me after one year, "I don't need you". As you will read in Chapter 3. My second wife said to me after three months "I don't feel you." And now, shortly after the second of 25 years of marriage, my third wife is telling me "I don't hear you".

The dynamics of our union were that in her home there were four children by two men, a grandmother and her alcoholic husband. On my side there were three children by two women. one of which was my first wife and two kids. At times there were a total of 10 people in our home. What an enormous challenge to undertake especially after I had recovered from the devastating loss of my third business and dream. Joyful Star Child Development Center of five years. There was a social worker who attended our church (my first church), who pulled me aside one Sunday alone. She said to me that while it was commendable of me to marry and care for this family, don't try and be a hero. The task is huge and you can't do it by yourself. She said that there are government resources that can be a great help. Utilize them and I did. My three children were very concerned that this family had taken away their father. They were very skeptical about sharing me. As were many others in and outside of my family, considering the traumatic experience I had just overcome.

I will share more about that experience in Chapter 9.

But I had just faced 40 years in prison, sued for 36 million dollars and was on trial for eight days. I had exhausted over $100,000 in legal fees. I assured my three children that I could handle the responsibility. They would not be slighted. I asked for their trust and support and to help me blend all of these Dynamics into a harmonious whole. Very reluctantly they agreed. I was free. Debt-free. I Owed no one anything. I had $25,000 in my savings account and was earning $1,000 per week. No car notes and no rent and I surrendered it all to and in my marriage to my third family. My wife's children's fathers Did not like me in any sense of the imagination and I never could understand why. I got up at 3:30 a.m. every day to go to work in my taxi, which was quite dangerous in those days. Sometimes during the day over 40 people were sitting behind me leaving me open and vulnerable to all kinds of robberies and attacks. If I made $200 in a day, $198 were spent on my wife's family household and the children of men who did not like or respect me. I honestly do not recall either of her children's fathers spending a minute or a dollar on them for 25 years. Instead of hating me, I thought they should be sending me weekly thank you cards. Sometimes things were so tight that if I did not go to work one day, something got disconnected. Pressure like you can't imagine. My children rarely required much of me because of their age. Their mothers had legal custody and my youngest daughter was in the Army for 20 of those 25 years of marriage. She is now fully retired after both Iraqi Wars. Thanks be to God. All of my money, time and energy were spent on my non-biological children. However, stepchildren or stepfather were terms not allowed in our home. I was not a step and I was not to be stepped on. If anyone was to be referred to as a step, it should have been the real fathers. I'm just saying. For real. In the eyesight of God and my marriage vows, all of my children are all of my children and all were treated equally barring no respect of parental responsibility. I never showed any favoritism even to my own. However, this was not the case in reverse. In my naivety,"don't hate – appreciate" Say thank you. However, that never happened with my wife's children's father and rarely with her children to this day.

My father had been an alcoholic for 47 years and I vowed that I would never follow that course or ever live with one again. But there I was because of my unconditional commitment to my wife, totally engaged in that behavior and lifestyle. Once again, my life was subject to the embarrassment and pain that I had experienced all of my life growing up. Her grandmother's husband, totally inebriated and helpless, had to be picked up off of the street wherever we were informed by police or strangers or neighbors who found out where he lived. Driving drunk and his car being taken from him by the authorities was a norm. Once he made it home without the new car he and his wife had purchased. She asked me if I could try and locate the car and hide it from him and I did. I hid the car at my sister's home in Maryland in their garage. When her husband awoke the next day and couldn't find it, he reported it stolen. She refused to tell him that she had asked me (the preacher) to hide it. The auto had a LoJack system installed and was easily tracked. When my brother-in-law called and informed me that the Prince George's County Sheriff was at his home I took full responsibility so that he and his wife would not be held accountable for Grand Theft Auto. I asked his wife to explain her rightful request as an owner to her husband and the police, but she refused in fear of her husband and not me facing 15 years in prison. Not realizing that I had been issued a summons to report to court because when it came in the mail, he destroyed it. An act of love, compassion and kindness for my wife's family and all of my good being made evil, now faced 15 years in prison. Shortly after this I was visited by the Metropolitan Police Department while my daughter watched me get arrested as a fugitive from Justice for Grand Theft Auto which carried a maximum of a 15-year sentence. And no one in my wife's family seemed to be so terribly alarmed. His alcoholic lifestyle ultimately led to her physical demise and death.

After being tried on the matter and released, after spending a night in jail, I refused to allow him access to the home we lived in. Because he was my wife's grandfather-in-law and her grandmother wanted her husband back in the home, this created much friction and animosity against me by my wife and her children who understandably loved their grandmother and were affected by her concerns regarding my unfairness, not my sacrifices for them or possible incarceration, but my unfair treatment to an alcoholic. What a life I've lived! Even though I faced 15 years, I suppressed my pride and dignity as a man and yielded to the emotions and pain of my family. SOMEBODY SAY AMEN…...At this point these sacrifices and unselfish challenges are becoming humanely overwhelming.

In the process of time, it was becoming evidently clear that this family's loyalties to each other, at whatever cost, was superseding any vows in marriage, promises, or acts of unification or sacrifices that I was making to enhance the quality of life I faced upon arrival or assignment. My wife's mother left her family home to her and her sister and brother. Right in the midst of her struggles as a mother with very limited resources and four minor children, they demanded their share of ownership which could only be possible if she sold the home. this would leave them with no place to live. While I apologize for my position, for the house was legally there's also. By no means was I going to stand by and allow them to be homeless. It was an ugly battle but I took total responsibility and needless to say even among my wife and children, my respect and integrity was questioned and scarred. A strong and confident Spirit of an angel of God in development was being diminished in quality and quantity by the day, the month, and the years. But like a tree planted by the water, I was not to be moved. I often wonder when I'm standing at Heaven's Gates, the only real wrong that can be attached to my life is a periodic intake of pink Moscato. Praise God for Sutter Home. Not perfect, but constantly perfecting. What else? How much more?

Standing again for what I believed was right and totally sensitive to the needs of others and being scrutinized for their sake and blamed for their fate and unfortunate realities was becoming all too real to imagine. It was beginning to sound like the Savior whose life I was trying to mimic. Crucified by those you're willing to give your life for. So far there was nothing really tangible in this for me but the satisfaction of knowing that I loved Jesus.

Shortly into our marriage, my wife made it clear how important it was for her to finish the education she desired., but was seriously hampered by her unsuccessful marriage. Understanding clearly, my biblical role as the man (head), my desire for someone I love and admire and of course, the answer to her Letter to God, I was moved or even compelled or maybe even mandated to bring resolve and make it happen. Either scenario was just fine by me. Remember my identity and purpose when I left home at sixteen. Add to it, the symptoms of children of alcoholic parents. I recalled the words spoken to me by the social worker

at our church. Don't be a hero. There are resources available to help you make this happen. I had not experienced any need for any public assistance programs in my life notwithstanding "welfare" during my childhood. Doing for others is an inspiration deeply embedded in my core. Even though it has brought me consistent loss and pain. She could not afford school, couldn't take off from work, had no one to care for her four children and no medical coverage for her family. Many of our associates had already assumed that she was the recipient of some form of government assistance but she was not until I came along. Truth be told. Isn't that awesome? Your deliverer, your knight in shining armor, your angel from heaven is here with your complete welfare package.

Here was my offer: You go to school and receive whatever level of education you desire and whatever is necessary to operate this family I'll take care of it. Wow! Now that I have gone through it, I must ask myself the question," what in the hell were you thinking". Here was the system I implemented: someone needed to be at home when the children were not in school. She saw the children off in the morning before she left for college which is where she was until late in the midnight hour or coming in at two or three in the morning when I was leaving for work. She was in class, cramming or studying with classmates. I left for work cabbing at 3:30 a.m. and worked until the children came home from school around 3:30 p.m. I cooked dinner for all four or five years straight. I took the children to choir rehearsal or Bible study, I assisted with homework and chores. I talked to them about all of their issues and conducted most Monday night mandatory family meetings. In those family meetings they were taught how to manage money, balance check books, the contributions blacks and whites made to life as we know it, and issues in the world, to name a few.

She attended college for seven years and only started working again after her second degree. She received a Bachelor of Arts (BA) degree and a Master's degree in biblical studies. Although I was only a high-school dropout, I knew how to listen. The government provided $380 in cash monthly. They provided all of our food stamps and complete family medical coverage. We got off Public Assistance after our educational mission was accomplished. I wanted somehow to say thank you to the church member who encouraged me to swallow my pride and ask for help. but she passed away in the process.

As the children grew Older there were times when there were three people in college at the same time. We received much assistance from grants for the children but all of my wife's tuition was out of pocket. All of our children had cell phones for contacts and security reasons, and on many occasions, they had friends who were less fortunate and had phones on our plan. We were barely hanging on and still carrying others. There were times when our cell phone bill reached $800 per month. I was totally immersed in the mission, the promise, the unconditional love, and the Mandate that drove me from the age of 16. Meeting everyone placed in my path at their needs. I was immersed in the expectations and needs for others, sacrificing when I was getting nothing in return at home and in church trying to do all that I thought God required of me. Selfless and consumed in the saying "if God was willing to die for me, then I will be willing to live for him." And it was beginning to kill me. It was beginning to drain me and diminish the quality of life He promised me. But he did not give up on me, so I just kept it moving, not realizing that the day was approaching when I would receive evil for my good even in

my third family for 25 years. I would receive total disappointment, pain, abandonment and an ungrateful recompense for all of my labor. I felt dis-eased spiritually, disease physically, Hepatitis C, walking pneumonia, high blood pressure, diabetes, sciatic nerve, blocked artery, cirrhosis of the liver, heart murmur, and chronic kidney disease. All had infiltrated my physical body and tried to take me out.

Satan, the Devil, comes at unawares in the midnight hours of life, seeking whom he may devour. In the beginning of our friendship, relationship and marriage, my wife and I seemed to be a perfect blend. I would assert that if it had not been for church and children we may have survived. As our activities in church increased and our children developed, our disagreements and philosophies became more challenging. It seemed to me that we reached a point when jealousy, envy and competition were creating a dominating undercurrent in our lives and any matter involving me outside of home were fueling our interactions and controlling our destinations. Every move I made was being scrutinized and everybody that got close to me or became an essential player in my life was attacked. These spirits also filtered over in all three churches I was a part of. I admit, I've always drawn a lot of attention, not because I was handsome, or well-endowed as a man or a player. Most of the work that I've done especially in my Christian life since 1980, I've tried to do it in a way that I thought would be pleasing to God. After all he said, "do all things to his glory". Subsequently when you please God, there's blessings, fruit and growth. People often draw to you when you are simple, sincere and genuine. Pastors have asked me to perform tasks and when I do good it is well accepted and spoken of. And it creates an issue when I become more popular than the leader. I'm real.

I'm not fake. They want to benefit from what I do but they attack me when I'm famed. Go figure! Often, I've concluded that if you don't want it done right or good, don't ask me to do it. I don't know any other way. Sometimes in my family's case I became a possession. Something they feared losing so they would subconsciously seek to destroy anything or anybody that got close to me. And while I was an angel from heaven, their pride would not let them say it. Their fear wouldn't let them risk losing it. It is a spirit that even early into our relationship was working against my growth and development as a businessman and leader in church. As the first family of the church, they would judge and condemn anyone that got close to me or that I needed that took them out of the limelight or center of my attention. It would become an immediate threat unless of course they befriended or liked someone. I could not operate or control God's Church based on my family's likes and dislikes of people. I was trapped. Sometimes set up. It's been a constant battle that has plagued my life especially in church. In my third church where I pastored, Shammah Ministries, in order to secure finances to support the ministry, which was small and struggling, we conducted banquets, weddings, receptions and repasts as a professional service to our members and the general public. It's called rent. In the state of Maryland anyone handling food had to be a licensed caterer and or have a state provided food handling license. We also catered these events two to three times per month and as a pastor, it was a vital resource in paying this shopping center rent. We were blessed of course to have on our staff, a licensed deacon and professional caterer with 20 years of experience. She also had all of the necessary equipment saving the church a lot of money (operating cost). What a blessing. My wife's daughter wanted the

job but was not fully equipped as a professional licensed caterer. She was not equipped with the essential supplies to carry out the magnitude we needed nor the license necessary. As the first family and watching the pastor's struggles to make it all happen, utilizing every resource available which is an essential support of the first family of a church, my wife and daughter threatened to disconnect from the church because I did not choose her. They threatened to leave me in the midst of a serious struggle in ministry and accuse me of being in an affair with the caterer. My wife's loyalties were not in support of her husband's mission as the first lady but was satisfying the inappropriate and unprofessional request of her child.

At the end of 2004, 30 of us, family and friends were led to start a church after we left the second church, we attended for four years. We believe that after all of our experiences, we could build God a church that he would be pleased with. While my family was a part of this founding mission, it wasn't until all of our children graduated from school that I felt free now to raise up a household of faith as God had inspired me to raise up my family. I placed no mandate or requirements on anyone in my family to be responsible for such an enormous undertaking. The call was mine not theirs, however if out of love and loyalty of family, they were willing to support the mission, I accept. Their behavior as we progressed was often displeasing to me as a pastor. They began to work against the order, principles, doctrine and compassionate spirit that God gave me for his people. They talked about, looked down on, condemned and judged the very people God called me to love unconditionally, teach, embrace and save. What an opposing force that begins to work against me and the successful development of a household of faith. Matthew 12:28 *Decrees that A house divided against itself shall not prosper.* My job as their Shepherd was to do the same for them as I had done for my own, that's why I waited until I had done all that I was assigned to do for my own before I accepted that awesome and time-consuming role as a shepherd. I put my family first and they demanded to stay there at whatever cost, to my desire or needs. After all, the criteria for leading God's church is found in 1 Matthews 3-8, if anyone does not know how to manage his own family, how can he take care of God's Church? My underlining opposition was doing what my family thought and wanted me to do and not what God required me to do for his people. It was always all about them and no one else took precedence over that.

Shortly after I lost my church of 15 years, and my family of 25 years, one of my most loyal members passed away. She was hurt because she could not save our church. She was hurt because she could not stop my fall. I will never forget her. It seems that as soon as she received my email notice to the church regarding its inability to continue, she died. I felt like I killed her because I failed. My wife and three daughters attended that funeral. I was hurt, and overwhelmed, sobbing like a baby, choked up and couldn't talk, alone, disillusioned and clearly at one of the lowest points in my life. and they sat there, in that church, after 25 years of total devotion in their lives, and watched me as if their eyes were saying, you deserve everything that's happening in your life. The fact is that they had caused much of everything that was happening in my life. No compassion, no loyalty not an ounce of sensitivity, just let me see you work your way out of this one. As If I had done them an injustice. I was distraught. Lord, how long? How much more?

During our tenure as a Christian Church, struggling, my wife's son

offered to help with two projects. I was skeptical at his request and explained that so many people offer to take on projects in the church and walk away without notice leaving me the added responsibility and the task of disappointing members when ministries fail. He assured me that he would not do that to me or God's Church. One of those ministries was a teacher and youth leader to my youth and young adult classes and they lived and loved to see him every Sunday. Her son got married and one Sunday morning without notice, he informed us that that was his last Sunday at our church. I asked if this decision is effective immediately and looking down, he said I have to talk to my wife. I waited a few days for a response which I never received. His mother felt that I was unfairly holding her son back from starting a new life, because I approached him as a young professional with ethics and protocol. In anger I asked him to leave what I thought at the time was our home and I expressed to him that as leaders of God's church, we deserved the same respect that he gave his previous employers, at least a two-week notice which he clearly had no intention of doing. Requiring my son to do things decently and in order was met with opposition by his mother, the First Lady of the church. I was faced with a church filled with disappointed teens and young adults. I have not seen him since or heard from him, but my desire would be, that you respect your new pastor more than you respected your father.

On the day that he and his wife moved his things, he caused the basement, my man cave and office to be flooded with water. The entire carpet in that room was soaked with puddles of water where I prepared all of my sermons. I shared that scene with his mother, and she informed me that he had just spilt a little container of water, despite the damage to her home and that I should stop attacking and accusing her son. She slept in that basement with me and for two months because of allergies, she could not stay down there because of the mildew smell. But she defended her child and accused me of over exaggerating. She visited the room and could not breathe because of the unbearable mildew odor and her asthma. She said that as a man, father, and head of house, I shouldn't hold my black son accountable for providing the same professional etiquette he showed a worldly business to God's church or his parents who led it. She literally accused me of hindering her son from starting a new life. Once again, she showed totally dangerous loyalty to her son, not the professional expectations of her husband, despite the damage he did to her home. His new life and wife divorced him shortly thereafter. I knew then that our marriage was unraveling. Revenge, I surmised for when I put him out at age 13.

I received a call from Barnard Elementary School that her son was in the middle of the floor on his back break dancing and the teacher had no control. I had received several complaints of his totally unacceptable Behavior, but this time I thought I would surprisingly show up. He was so preoccupied with his activity that neither the teacher nor the students could get his attention and point out his father looking through the door. When we arrived home, I asked him to call his biological father to come and pick him up because in 30 minutes he and all of his belongings would be outside on the front porch. When he called his father wanted to speak to me. He informed me that I wasn't his father and I couldn't put him out no matter what he did. You remember how hard I worked to care for these children? I asked him: "So, I have to take whatever your son dishes out to me at the age of 13?" In some not so pleasant words to a

preacher, he said "yes". I put him out and of course my ethics were as a man of God scrutinized, not his son's behavior. He told his son that day, I'm coming to get you now. His son was 13 then and maybe 35 now and I don't believe he has shown up yet. His mother went to get him when she arrived home from school after 10 p.m. or so. She had heard from all of the other relatives and upon entering the home she asked me, so what should I do now? I said to her, "we need to go and get him before there's any further damage done to him." Remember, I'm unorthodox, technical, and complex. I had no intention of leaving him there. I needed to make a point to the whole family. I put my life in danger every day providing for his children. Don't play with me. I'm not the one. Revenge is yet another deep-rooted spirit that flows into this family's bloodline. Her son also walked away from the second project he vowed to uphold at his parents' church.

I am constantly reminded of the letter that I wrote my mother and the mission I vowed to undertake at the age of 16. Additionally over the 25 years I was married, I was equally determined to uphold her request to God, for our God and complete all expectations and assignments to the best of my ability. However, I submit at this point in my life, the challenges and oppositions were becoming quite overwhelming and bleak. When my wife and I married, I had but two requests, that she remained faithful to me and never put her children before me as our vows required. I have kept every promise I made to her and she has broken every promise she made to me, excluding being faithful. Women often err, in the eyesight of God and their marriage vows (forsaking all others) when they take the position that no man comes before my children. This is the most dangerous and blatant error that occurs in

God's institution, probably only second to infidelity. While, it yet seems an honorable and obvious disposition, even by virtue of the nine months I carried you, it is us first and them and not them first and then us. I pray that many who read this book would have a constructive and sensitive dialogue on this issue. This concept would or should only apply in the context of marriage. My children and her children were always second and she, her dream and her relationship with her God was always my priority. Those matters being in order simply makes for a wonderful journey raising a family as one. I trust you will try that Because our children will play us against each other to the very end, and in my case, they will destroy us. I am confident she loved me to a fault. She cared for my mother when my own brothers and sisters wouldn't or couldn't. She spent all eight days in court with me when I was accused of abusing children and lost my business. But it was clear that her priority and total loyalties were to her four children, even when they were completely wrong and out of order. Because I put her first and gave her all, I expected nothing less in return. If her children had opposition, she had opposition. They disrespected and regulated her all the time and threatened and expected her to side with their issues or concern simply because she was their mother. It became increasingly incarcerating to operate our home, church or any business I engaged in as our children grew up and our social and financial involvement expanded with these phenomena at play. When her son (her youngest child) went to Pittsburg State University he was accompanied by an AT&T, $17,000 credit card to ensure he had access to all he needed. This security blanket was paid in full at the end of his tenure there and he has yet to ask or inquire how much it cost over four years.

That's how I rolled with responsibilities that were not mine. You expect more from anybody, when you give more to anybody. The biblical Foundation says, to whom much is given, much is required. Her middle-aged daughter went to Temple University. When we went to enroll her, we were informed that her housing arrangement had not been taken care of. She insisted that she handled the matter. She had not. At that time, I had begun to migrate out of the 38 years of driving a taxicab. Unfortunately, that process ceased. I purchased another taxi so that her one-bedroom rent would be secured for four years. At this time, my three children did not require any assistance from me, and her children were exhausting every resource available.

I will share the significance of this point later in Chapter 9---

The Bible declares that "they shall know the truth and the truth shall make them free. I sincerely love my family, but over the years we have exemplified some character traits and practices that does not embody my call to serve God's people and has caused irreparable damage to those we were assigned to heal, help and honor. Jesus said that what you do unto the least of these my children, you do also unto me. Vengeance, selfishness, rage, insensitivity, jealousy, Envy, control, judging, condemning, and belittling have plagued my life and the first family of the church we erected to bring God glory. I take full responsibility. I have Incorporated these experiences of my life because I truly loved my family and I truly believe the truth shall make us free. It has been said that all things that are done in darkness, shall come to light and whatever you do to others, works its way back to you. I believe every word that is written in God's divine instrument. I pray that you are enlightened by the truths and do not remain in darkness concerning yours.

As time progressed, my challenges and attacks on my identity and purpose became even more paramount. The reality of losing became more probable and complex, testing my ethics, integrity and expectations, or being held accountable for other's actions.

My wife's oldest child became married. In the tenth year of her marriage, it was revealed to me that my son-in-law had been in an outside affair that resulted in the birth of two children. Our church was small and only five years old. The news devastated our home and church. We were truly on the verge of destruction. He came to me as a pastor and shared in confidence their situation and intent. My son-in-law was a licensed deacon and served as a spiritual leader in the church. You can begin to understand the immediate impact. The couple did not choose to share this knowledge with the mother but strictly in confidence with me, the stepfather and pastor. My wife was outraged and angry with me (the pastor) because I held fast to my ethics and even though it was her daughter, I was bound to honor their request. This concept or expectation in managing the church has caused many dilemmas and attacks on my character. I am not at Liberty to show favoritism or impartiality to anyone in God's house, as he does not, and my family has constantly attacked me for doing so. God is not a respecter of persons. We are all equal in his sight. At home they are our family and their needs and concerns are our priority. My life as pastor and father was torn between distinctions for the 15 years I served as a leader. My wife was severed because of this act against her child. Our children were mixed with anger, hurt and disappointment with their sister when she decided

to forgive her husband and remain in the marriage. Honorable in God's sight but totally unacceptable among her siblings. She said her reason was because of how I had raised her, that I had been teaching forgiveness for a year and the situation had the potential of destroying everything that I had worked to build. This was one of the few doctrines and examples of Christian Living that we as the first family truly exemplified. Strangely enough the church's major focus on this matter was not on my wife's daughter nor her husband's infidelity. It was on me and how I was going to handle this sensitive and intricate sin activity in comparison to how I process similar nonfamily matters. I chose to preach on the power of the forgiveness of sin for one month, in part to put out the fire. The fact is that I held in confidence what would have released me from scrutiny. The attack and expectations on my sacred oath of office and unnecessary damage to family and church is this, the husband and wife had been in agreement with this affair the entire five years because of her painful unwillingness to please her husband sexually. We literally and deeply hated a man that was given permission by his woman. Once again, there I was, trapped by my own integrity and loyalty from saving myself and my dream from utter destruction by honoring and respecting the needs and will of others. My credibility among those I'm called to serve, permanently scarred for holding others in an esteem above myself. Giving and sacrificing even when it's killing me to do so. Mind you, that I had transferred $40,000 worth of debt from them that they had accrued so that they could purchase a home and return the funds when it was comfortable for them to do so. What's love got to do with that? Acts of a stepdad?

Later I will share with you how she walked out of my life totally inconsiderate of how I had walked(served) in hers.

And they shall know the truth, and the truth shall make them free.

My wife's youngest daughter aspired without a doubt to be an actress since she was four years of age. We spent most of her life making sure she was connected to every school and resource to ensure she reached that goal. Duke Ellington School of the Performing Arts and Rutgers State University to name a few. As her life progressed it was suggested that her main gift was in the field of directing and not acting. She was truly good I admit but all too often practiced her gifts on the stage of our home, and her family. One day as we sat in the kitchen, we heard a loud and angry shout at her brother. I rushed to the scene on the stairway. She shouted with such a deep penetrated and convinced anger, "STOP" and called his name. The problem was that her brother had done absolutely nothing to her, nor had he said anything to her. He was shocked. she wanted to get him into trouble with me, so she performed that stunt to perfection. She was good and still is. She literally presented a convincing stage performance so effective that it got her brother into trouble. She exacted the art of acting as far back as I can remember from the age of four when I married her mother. As she grew older she became shrewd, manipulating, cunning, vengeful, insensitive, inconsiderate, selfish and like her almost twin brother, arrogant and self-centered. Each of our children were different and though we were struggling, I did all I knew to do to help them identify and live in the experience of what they aspired to do. Her youngest daughter took this platform and opportunity to the highest power at every opportunity that she could. As our children grew older, I never got involved in their sibling rivalry, this child demanded favoritism and special treatment. I would often get into trouble with the

entire family for allowing her to use our home environment as her practice ground. I was often accused of showing her favoritism and letting her get away with murder. Boy did I screw that up? I must admit that I was intrigued with her determination to go to Hollywood and I may have been a little more lenient toward her and was prepared to ultimately support her living in Hollywood close to those she aspired to be like. I was this way with all of our children but admittedly this one was" off the hook".

Well into her adulthood, one day she returned home from a tour in Oklahoma and informed me that she was pregnant. As a father, I suppose, I became a bit alarmed that this was the result of my daughters one-night affair. She always informed me that she was not like my other daughters (with children, not virgin), and would not disappoint her father, the pastor. Such an intriguing and impressive personality? As offensive as it was, I understood what she was trying to say. This news alarmed me because of the lifestyle and activities she assured me she was not engaged in. Like any parent, I tried to trust my children! As a result, I found her news to be a little concerning and that she was considering a future with this man quite older than she was. In our church at the time there were nine babies born over a period of 15 months. Most of them were single mothers with two or three children. All of their circumstances were painful, unplanned and sometimes embarrassing. Most of them had no fathers in the homes where they were raised. As their pastor, father, brother and friend, the responsibility to love them, embrace them and nurture them was overwhelming for me considering I had seven children under my wings in our family. During this time my wife, daughters and siblings would make fun of all of these young ladies. They would constantly condemn, judge and ridicule them regarding their Christian lifestyle Even in our home, often publicly and moreover in my presence as their pastor. So, I found the news of my wife's daughter's pregnancy to be quite contrary. She called them on occasion, booty snatchers making booty calls, whores, Girl Friday, forced and compelled with baby daddy drama. And now she finds herself having to publicly face those same unfortunate realities and, acting and perpetrating became the performances of a lifetime. Eating crow is such a nasty delicacy. Protecting her image became the most evil, destructive and devastating pursuit of a lifetime. Stage front and with Oscar and Emmy possibilities. Snapped. It in fact destroyed a 15-year church and a 25-year marriage. Baby daddy drama was no longer an issue with the little girls at church, it was in the pastor's home corrupting everything that I hoped and thought we had built.

My wife's daughter was in serious trouble now at this point. Pride, anger, rage, vengeance and her image was totally consuming her life and she was on a" by any means necessary" mission to protect it from the same slander, condemnation and vile judgment that she verbally and publicly inflicted and exhibited toward all of the single girls at church with" baby daddy drama". She had now proven publicly that she was engaged in the same "BOOTY CALLS", That she was a little" HO", just like them. She could not face this new image of herself, that she had hidden so well and was now at War to preserve her credibility. Psychologists are alarmed at what a vengeful personality will do in anger and rage. As always, Somebody or something had to cover and protect her integrity. She had to get this monkey off of her back. Somebody had to pay for what she, in this case, did to herself and somebody had to be

blamed. As low of an act that it was, she chose the pastor, the First Lady (her mama) and the church to put on the performance of her life. Of course, that is where she condemned herself in condemning others. In this case that would be her stepfather, her mother and her entire family to restore her deeply tarnished reputation and image. She used all of us.

A baby shower at her church and she invited every girl that she had condemned to hell as trash. She had to show them that she was pure and acceptable but they were trash. That's sick. She was now spoiled goods, sinful, dirty and was about to use everyone she could to attend her strategic presentation and display of HOLINESS. It was lavish, elaborate, professional and very glamorous. She invited all of the eloquent, elite and important people in our family, friend and church inner circle. A red-carpet affair. I was yet again in an awkward position as father and pastor. A no-win situation, to do what I could not do but was compelled to do because of the misconceptions I faced by all if I did not participate. As a pastor, I was obligated to operate God's Church according to his biblical instructions and spiritual insight. God's word is clear regarding sex out of wedlock and the perceptions of how you were looked upon. I could not give the impression that I condone this behavior by anybody, while at the same time, I was their spiritual leader and obligated to embrace love and support them in spite of their issues. All have sinned and come short of the glory of God, starting with me. For even while I was sinning, Christ died for me. This is why judging others can be devastating to your own health. Jesus said I did not come to condemn, but that by me and thru me all would be saved. I did not participate in all of the other little girls' baby showers(and they understood), most held at their church, but my stepdaughter was determined to have me present and to present this authentic, honorable and acceptable front to reflect that she was special because her father and mother were the pastor and first lady. It's hard, but pastors must draw a line in what they support and embrace especially if it's in opposition to the word, the will, and the way of God. I assisted in setting it all up but before the invited guests arrived, I left. I assisted in setting it up because of the limited staff that I had, I set up most events that we accommodated. I helped my family set it up because I was the father and it was the appropriate thing to do, however there was another set of principles that I honored. Torn between two loves. Out of all fairness in God's house, I would not do special favors for my child that I wouldn't do for the other girls. My image and reputation were also on stage and the person who was watching my performance was God.

My leaving shattered my stepdaughter. My wife and her children didn't regard me for months. They could not use God's elect as a pond or a prop to taunt and humiliate any of God's children, in particular these other girls. I am confident that no one knew or understood my behavior in this season but me and the God I love and serve. She wanted me, in the presence of all in attendance, to make her" sinful act" seem okay and acceptable. Authenticate her wrong and condemn others. Her vengeance now was in full Pursuit against me and exacting payback was multiplied. Turning my wife, her mother against me, the members and her brother and sisters were part of her agenda and lying, deceiving, manipulation were her tools. Weapons of choice. To this day her vindictive spirit is rampant and comfortable in its accomplishments and her family can't break from her power over them.

She is the equivalent of a vicious animal that will attack without

notice or compassion for their prey. I was always moved by her beautiful smile, but behind it was the spirit of a pit bull, not to be trusted under absolutely no circumstances, and at no point in time. Her mere presence traumatized her family, but not mine. That was a serious challenge for her, performing on a stage when half of the attendees did not appreciate your agenda. She possessed a narcissistic personality disorder. She was toxic(poison) to anyone who did not agree with her. And she had a Passive Aggressive Personality. That means, when she wanted to attack you, and had no justifiable reason, she created a scene or situation in which she could Now respond accordingly. To carry out what she really wanted to do all the time. That's sick, but that's ACTING. This state of mind, landed me often to the question," can God really change the heart of man?" Under his authority, I thought that I had the ability to change, correct, or redirect these into a more positive use. After all, I had come to believe that meeting the needs of this family is why he sent me there. The Bible says," be ye transformed by the renewing of your mind". Renewing your mind invites an action that is required of you. It requires a choice one makes within themselves and not an outer force regulating their behavior. Choose ye this day. The Free Will choice to change lies within.. The result of that is the power of God working in you. According to the power that worketh in you or according to the power that you invite and allow to work in you (Ephesians 3:20). Can God or will God force himself on you? She has not changed and will not change until she acknowledges, like an alcoholic, that there is even a need for her to change. How many lives will suffer until that day is upon us? This evil spirit is comfortable in its skin. It thrives on its ability to wreak havoc on others at will, for reasons it contends are justified.

Again, I guess that I can admit that her smile captured my heart along with her sincere desire for Hollywood and her ability to perform(act). Under normal circumstances, those are all attributes that can contribute to one's success, but she has failed. Her biggest failure is her mother because she refused to use her influence in her daughter's life to contribute to her change, she simply accepted and defended her behavior which further empowered her.

Uncontrollable rage grasps the mental ability to think clearly and rationally and will even use God to annihilate its opponents. It limits one's ability to live a life of purpose and value. It cares nothing about truth, facts, or its contributions to a matter. It owns nothing. It simply passes on all of its vices and venom to someone or something else. It is always in a preoccupied state of existence, subconsciously pursuing a vendetta.

The Bible shares many thoughts on this mindset. Do unto others as you would have or want others to do unto you. Matthew 7:12. Whatsoever a man soweth, that shall he also reap. Galatians 6: 7. All things done in darkness, shall come to light. Luke 8:17. judge not; for what you judge with, you will be judged by. Matthew 7:1. What you put out is coming back and seven times worse than when you administered it. When my wife's daughter arrived home from the tour in Oklahoma, she assured me it was not a one-night affair. Please keep in mind that this child was an adult and in no way accountable to me. She told me that her baby daddy would be coming to see me and talk to me like men did in the old days, requesting their daughter's hand in marriage. She said he's a good man. He cares a lot for me. We are taking a trip to Florida to look for our home so the baby will be raised close to our family instead of his.

He wants to do the right thing, dad. She wanted me to accept him into our family, love him and embrace him as one of us. As the leader of our family she asked me. While I was somewhat hesitant to honor her request, she pleaded my support and involvement with her future husband. I gave in, against my better judgement, and as so many men, when it comes to their precious little girls. A syndrome that often leaves father's disappointed at the midnight hours of life, but love keeps us together for life. He has been on his way to see me, to discuss those matters since early 2018 and as I write this chapter, it's May of 2021.

He did not show up to discuss their plans as she had informed me, but I did receive a call. My wife's daughter was not aware that I had proceeded to do what she asked me, and embrace her baby daddy into our home. She had cut me out of the picture and my children, so there was no interaction. I met the young man at a restaurant and I shared four concerns with him:

1. I apologized for my daughter's behavior.

2. When this is over and under control, you will forgive her and treat her like it all never happened.

3. No matter what happens, my granddaughter needs her father. I expect you to take full responsibility for your child and care for her and provide her the best quality of life that she deserves.

4. Lastly, I told him that I was aware that his mother was a pastor of a church. I know that you really don't like what I am telling you but, I am sharing with you, young man, what Jesus Christ is expecting of you regarding this situation. And if you fail to provide that child proper care, I will disown you.

In all actuality I was not only carrying out her request, I was really helping her for her baby and take care of her. I knew that he thought I was crazy, he revealed that to me, but I was doing what I was called by God to do and that's minister the doctrine and principles of Jesus Christ, in season and out of season. Whether you like or want to do it or not, as my servant. As I have shared, the Bible says in all that you get, get understanding. Do not act on perception or assumptions, get the facts. But when you allow evil to entrap you, you become subject to the powers therein, and you are no longer able to see the Light of the Glorious Gospel of Jesus Christ. The TRUTH. And you walk in darkness. The young man whom I didn't know stated when he called that, he did not mean me or my family any disappointment or trouble. He apologized to me in tears. He sounded very choked up and nervous. He said that he and my wife's daughter we're on the highway to Florida to look for a home. She asked me while I was driving about my opinion involving a dear friend of hers in California and how she was mourning the death of her mother. He said I simply responded after she insisted on my opinion, that you can't regulate how your friend is mourning her mother's death and get upset with her because she did not consult your way first. He was in the car when my wife's daughter got into an argument with her friend and overheard their discussion. He told me, your daughter was quiet and then all of a sudden, she became a raging animal. and to yell at me and poke me in the head while I was driving. I asked her to stop before I had an accident and her rage and profanity increased. Sir, it was only my opinion. I simply disagreed with how she felt her friend should have respected her advice. He said, I am calling to tell you that what I experienced with your daughter was so frightening and shattering that I

decided I could not go through with our plan and I'm so deeply sorry if I caused your family and you any trouble. I pulled over and asked her to get out of my car and she refused. I promised her that if she just kept her hands off of me while I was driving, I would give her the car at the airport, but this is over. I will do everything in my power to assist and participate fully in caring for my daughter. My wife's daughter never informed me that those plans were totally canceled as I was attempting to move on her request. She did inform her mother and biological siblings. So, without being aware we were now two families working against each other instead of two families working together as I envisioned for 25 years. She strategically chose who she wanted to tell and what she wanted them to know not realizing that she was dividing our family. My daughters had informed her of their opposition to this relationship, so when it failed, she could not face them, she just simply began to block them from her life and wrapped all of her energy around those who she knew she could manipulate into seeing things from her perspective. Her loyalty now to her biological brother and sisters and her mother was now in full destructive mode and she simply erased me and my children from existence and her family enjoined her. She could not face me with the truth. The fact is that her plans were never genuine. They were simply a ploy to protect her image from family, friends and church and all of those little girls, but it backfired. When that cover-up failed, she would now be completely exposed to every element she spoke against them and her raging and vengeful behavior increased. She lied to her family and said that her baby daddy had hit her and told the court that the man had threatened to shoot her, but she needed to protect her image at whatever cost.

Being a married woman to cover for her biblically sinful acts were out and somebody had to pay. Again, the Bible says that a house divided against itself shall not prosper, and the pattern of my life from 16 years of age was about to become a reality again. Pure evil had now found another way to destroy me and my desire to show my mother a better way. My mother loves my wife, probably as much as she loves us, but because of dementia, she will never experience the evil and unfair treatment of her son, by her children. Her son who gave them his life.

My wife and children thought that they knew it all and were always willing to expose the infirmities and faults of others but went through painstaking measures to hide theirs. Her daughter became cunning and calculating, lying planting negative seeds against me because I would not join her and her family in crucifying an innocent man who simply wanted to do the right thing. One Sunday after church she tried to use my daughter to speak to her baby daddy on FaceTime in church to solicit information from him and when my daughter refused to be used, she viciously turned her rage on her. She called her family after the incident and spread lies to her own siblings about my daughter's actions. She used her baby on her hip as a shield to attack my daughter and her character. They were not there on the scene, but they believed their sister and all began to accuse and demean her. They blamed my daughter for destroying our family and church when she had separated from the family for 20 of the 25 years that we were married. She is a 20-year retired soldier who fought in both Iraq Wars and had simply refused to be used. They all knew their sister, the actor, her history growing up and they hinged their position on every word she spoke, even turning her against the man that raised them all. Their 25-year provider. When she thought that I was going to support her baby's daddy, she told all of my family that I had turned my loyalties to her baby's daddy and was prepared to testify against her in court and abandon my family. They believed her. I offered them proof from court documents that it was a lie and because of their loyalties to each other they rejected the proof and me. What price will you pay to defend evil? She went to court prepared to slander my credibility and use a resolved child abuse accusation to discredit me because now she does not want me around her child. I would have been a good grandfather by the way. She also presented in court a resolved murder case against my biological daughter to discredit her in open court. Her sister of 25 years. Rage, uncaged and out of control because a man did not like what he saw in her. One day when her baby's daddy and his wife returned the child from a weekend visit, my wife's daughter reached into the car and gashed his face with her nails, as his wife and daughter sat in the front seat watching. There is no limit to rage and vengeance. The court was not so concerned that she physically assaulted him first and sent him to the hospital but that his response was too excessive. The court admitted that it was her fault in that she provoked the incident but did not hold her accountable. She was out of control but he was expected to exercise self-discipline. That's called equal rights in America. He is facing criminal charges. Clearly it was a set up by the actor. Then she sends pictures to his superiors to have him fired all because he couldn't marry her because of her excessive personality.

Later, she and her older sister went to a range to take shooting lessons. While she was there she took a doctored photo from their physical encounter and showed it to the instructor. She asked him, if someone shot a person that did this, could they get away with it? She also immediately, after the incident called three of her cousins and showed them the photo and encouraged them (played on their sympathy) to track down her baby's daddy and kill him. Hidden rage in pursuit of vengeance and she used her older sister to help cover up the plot.

Their child is four years old. The father has spent all of two months with her in four years and he is fighting desperately now just to have a FaceTime conversation until it is all resolved, and the court rejected it. A black man trying desperately to be in his child's life and her mother at every turn depriving her of that relationship. And that would represent a third generation of women raised without a father. The curse continues. Rage, vengeance, payback, image. Her vindictive intent to control a man, force his choices deprive him of his honor and sincere desire to care for his child, using his child as a weapon and make him suffer for her own humiliation is insensitive and inhumane, all to exact control and destruction of a man's right to choose. My wife's daughter has used lawyers, judges, a court system, county criminal laws, her own mother, siblings, cousins, and a pandemic. All of my wife's children had no active father in their home until I came along. Sent by God and now a third-generation grandchild must suffer the same generational curse. While one of my wife's children was my godchild, this child benefited more from my unconditional love for family and total loyalty. Even to those I am not responsible.

Feeling defeated and detecting clearly now that my work with and for this family was rapidly coming to an end, my pressure was in the danger zone. My professional driver's license was being threatened. I prided myself over my years as a pastor and father on never giving up on people because God never gave up on me. However, resolve was nowhere in sight. My wife was totally loyal to her children. Put them above me. She believed every word and trusted every action they took in this unified effort to deprive a man from seeing his child even on FaceTime. The judge ordered that my daughter and I could not be anywhere close to this baby. My church was slowly failing and membership dropping because of their hidden negative influence. They stole $13,000 from my private area to obtain legal counsel in their pursuit to stop this father from getting close to his daughter and to make him suffer from rejecting her. They went into my phone to erase incriminating information so that they could continue to deceive me. After 25 years how much more did God require of me? How long could I hold on to a lifetime commitment to my wife and my God? Everything was working against me. All of her children distanced themselves from me. They had maintained a private group text among themselves for more than 12 years. They wanted me homeless, broke and my credibility with my members destroyed. They collectively conspired against me because as a father, pastor and fair and decent human being. I would not support these consistent acts of Vengeance and rage against someone else for what they had brought upon themselves. I was informed that I destroyed their family, that all that I was going through was my fault and I brought it all upon myself.

I deserve to suffer and lose all that I had worked so hard to accomplish, all over some baby daddy drama. On my last visit to the home that I resided for 25 years and was led to believe was owned with my wife, I asked her to support me, stand against this evil even if it involved our children because God required much more from us. I was crying and pleading desperately, unmoved by my pride and dignity as a man. She refused to face the facts. To tell the truth and advise her children that their behavior and actions were ungodly and unacceptable, but she and none of her children were ever strong enough to stand up against this daughter. That night I left my wife with no intention of ever returning again. I loved her child, I supported her child, and I believed in her child. I wrote this story in part and in hopes that a peer, a friend, a pastor or one of her own one day might be encouraged in spite of her bullying demeanor to help her. She is in serious trouble and the career we fought so hard to establish and secure for her is highly improbable. Our whole world was now at the behest of an angry vengeful and raging young black woman whose image among her peers, family and church had been shattered and there was nothing that I could do to stop it or help her. Three generations of women who were deprived of the balance that a loving father on the premises contributes to life. That balance, they had yet to experience, until I came along and they rejected it. And now there is a four-year-old precious little girl, that because of the insensitivity of a raging mother has to continue this curse and deprivation.

The basic tone of this book is not too attack or condemn anyone. It is to reflect the constant attacks on my life at every turn, since the age of 16, and how the opponent used everyone that crossed my path to reach his ultimate mission. That is to stop the work of the cross. That meant stopping me. I am in Christ, and Christ is in me profoundly. His cross is my cross. We are one. If he can destroy me, he can destroy Christ and his works. If he can destroy you, then he has successfully destroyed Christ. My problems came because I am one with Jesus Christ. I pray that Christians especially would get that, it is truly not about us. For we wrestle not against flesh and blood but spiritual wickedness in high

places. The devil, the enemy, and opposer wants to sift you like wheat (drain you of and from everything good or Godly) and by any means necessary he tried to stop me and seemingly succeeded every time. But, for God I'll live, and for God I will die, blessed be the name of the Lord. It's been just that real since I met Jesus in 1980. And I have the scars to prove it. Living the life that Jesus lived and desires that you try to do likewise, can often find you in a very lonely place, as it did him also. The Garden of Gethsemane was a very painful place for Jesus as he prepared to die on the cross, seven days later. As a human being he considered, let this pass from me. In other words, just thinking about the suffering is almost excruciatingly unbearable. However, I came to die so that others might live. and in the words of one of DC's finest, Marvin Gaye", LET'S GET IT ON"

I write this book in hopes that my life story will serve as an inspirational lesson to all who shall read it. Maybe you are confronted with this question today. How long can I survive in the environment that I am living in? How much damage has to be done before I drop this hot coal that's burning my hand to a crisp and causing permanent damage to all involved? When is it appropriate and intellectually necessary to walk away? The biblical definition of death is a slow, depleting, diminishing and deterioration of the quality of life that God promised us all. I was dying. Do I hold on and die, realizing that, or let go and live? On November 5, 2018, I let it go. To this day, I hurt, cry and beat myself up for failing God and the mission he assigned me at the request of my wife. As an Under Shepherd of Christ, that's how serious I took my work. because that's how serious he took his.

When my wife and I started out together, it seemed that our work and love for our God was a match made in heaven. I sincerely believe that it was, but the devil like a thief in the night comes to kill, steal and destroy. You know the story! However, as we grew in marriage, we grew apart as did our total cause to live for Christ and our commitment and call to serve his people above all else. What exactly do we mean when we say that we put Christ first in our lives, but our actions clearly indicate the opposite? We love God above all, but we put all above God. My wife's favorite scripture was Matthew 6:33, Seek ye first the kingdom of heaven, and all these other things will be added unto you. We were on the same page For in my heart I live and give for his great cause. However, to see Christ first in life is to apply his Doctrine to and in all things first. Measure everything against the Word. Come on, for real Pastor, who does that? As I shared with you, when I met Jesus and became aware of his love and doctrine, I was immediately sold out. I live to give as he did. And to that extent I've grown accustomed to sacrificing as he did. When I can't breed his love in my works, it chokes me, and I can't breathe. I can't thrive or survive. It's debilitating. But when I can, when I'm allowed, when I'm given the platform and provisions to perform his will and his work, it's invigorating and I can exhale and be purpose driven. Our priorities in life as a team slowly shifted directions.

In the midst of all, there came another opportunity to contribute and fulfill his desire to let Thy Kingdom Come on Earth as it is in heaven. To salvage and restore all who he died for. My wife's oldest daughter introduced me to an associate of hers. She wanted to know if I could help her. Isn't that awesome? Her children knew who I was and who I represented. After all it was clear that I helped them, and how. She was in despair, depressed and totally disillusioned. Her integrity and

Independence had literally collapsed and there was no hope in sight for her. She had three children, no job, her husband had completely abandoned them and he treated her worse than you would an animal.

All of our children had left home. Empty nest if you will. We had this great opportunity to serve God even in our home and at the request of her own child. I will never forget that moment that I continued as a servant of God to continue to perform his perfect will for us." I would that all men might be saved." She arrived at our home and I invited her in, and she sat quietly on the couch. She proceeded to try and talk to me about her state and status, but she just couldn't say a word. She was all choked up. She couldn't even explain her pain. I became her mouthpiece, her protector and her saving grace that day and for the next 15 months. She had only one desire at that moment and that was to regain her independence. She took great care of her children while in our home. She respected our home and my wife and was ever so grateful. I gave her money at my insistence, to get her nails done, fix her hair, dress up and go out periodically for a glass of wine and social activities. I don't think that she would mind me telling you that she was a real mess. I placed a monitor at her 18-month-old bedside so I could see every move and hear every sound that she made while her mother was away at night. She was not a member of our church yet. I gave her only two instructions. "Don't bring any more babies in our home and on the few nights that she went out, be in the house by 2:30 a.m., because I had to leave for work at 3:00 a.m. Her presence in our home required no responsibilities from my wife nor our children. I was fully responsible for her accommodations. We were on a mission to restore her decency and sanity and thanks be to God, we were meeting the task.

There came a time during this process that one of my wife's children decided she wanted to move back home. But clearly, because of our missionary work, there was no room in the Inn. Once again there were six people occupying our home and I guess there was no rest for the weary. The adult child that wanted to move back in was, of course, the actress. This intention was clearly met with opposition by me. I had done all that was desired and required of me as a father in preparing his children for adulthood and this opportunity to serve was welcomed by my heartfelt purpose to help others. My family's pursuit and intent became simply just to put this family out. Our priorities took light once again. My family's defense and argument were that this was our home and we should be able to access it at will. My position was that our home had been converted into a Haven of freedom and human dignity. A place of refuge, at their request.

My wife's daughters' assertions were that our guest was out making booty calls. My intent was that she not feel confined, trapped, limited and void of the basic human needs to engage in a social environment with her peers despite her limited resources and responsibilities. She was young and she was human, not on punishment in jail. As you can discern, my wife's daughter's pattern was to play her sexually immoral and ungodly booty call trump card to judge, condemn and discredit her prey. It was and has always been so transparent. This is the same booty call conundrum she made in Oklahoma that ultimately led to the painful destruction of our family and church. The tongue has the power to lift up or tear down. There is a cliche that says," Oh what tangled webs we weave, when at first we deceive." The tongue, your words are dangerous.

They are like a two-edged sword that cuts asunder, and tears into pieces. In the tongue, is the power of life and death. In your mouth is the power to build up or tear down. Our daughter used it most of her adult life to pierce and destroy anyone in her path for her own agenda or anyone who got in the way of her pursuit. Self-esteem had been her greatest challenge growing up and she would cut herself out of all of our family portraits, because she did not like the way she looked. Her mother's love often blinded her from recognizing the faults in her children for fear of confronting her own flaws and fears, or the perception thereof. CORRECTION IS PERFECTION, IT'S NOT AGAINST THE LAW All of our children and even many adults require it. It is a form of growth and development. No harm, no foul. She overlooks, overcompensates, justifies and tolerates her children's behavior, even when she knows it's wrong or seriously flawed. These were some of the depths of the challenges I faced as an outside father and pastor. These emotional, psychological and foundational issues often go undetected for a lifetime and destroys everything in their paths. They were all from a place of disrespect, rejection, abandonment and the damaging results had been permeated in their persona in spite of the fact that God had sent a Moses to deliver them.

Needless to say, the actress began her predictable pattern and typical pursuit, slander, discredit, condemnation and judgement. She didn't feel that the resident had a right to go out and have fun because of "all of them babies" and she was out on the town. I had clearly made sure that her mother was able to go out and have fun, even with all of her four babies.

Once again while trying to live out the true purpose of my calling, my ethics, principles and loyalties were questioned and translated into having an affair and "he must be hitting that," Accusations in my home then carried into my church, all because an adult Christian woman couldn't have her way and come back home where God was blessing another family the way he had blessed hers. My home, the pastor's home was failing at reflecting godly character in the church. I was trying to carry out the mandate of my calling and my heart's desire to please God in my work.

At every single turn in my life and ministry, my good was evil spoken of and used as a scapegoat for others agendas. As much opposition as I faced in my own home and as many permanent bruises that were being inflicted on my relationship with my wife and family, like a tree planted By the Waters I shall not be moved. And I tried so hard to be steadfast, unmovable, always abounding in the work of the Lord. 1 Corinthians 15:58. That young lady today has two Sons in college. She owns her own home. She has a beautiful career and is happily married. May the works that I have done, speak for me.

ONE WORD----ONE MISSION-----INDEPENDENCE

I was confident that we could take all of our family dysfunctions that we faced in the beginning and create a product that resembled the beautiful orchestration of a bouquet of flowers. All different colors, personalities, sizes and visions, uniquely arrayed that would be pleasing in God's sight and an example for all humankind to behold. Dr. Martin Dr. Martin Luther King called this phenomenon" transforming all of the disconnected aspects of reality into a harmonious whole'". A vision, not perfect but perfecting. Together we had the potential of making it happen. The divine reality of unconditional love and sacrifices. After all we were rooted and grounded in our love for Christ and his work. No greater foundation to build upon. That's how Jesus rolled, and that's how I was willing to roll for Jesus. My thing was and still is that if he was willing to die for me, I was willing to live for him, in life and in this union. The first order of business is that we were one. In the beginning, as her letter stated, it was about her. and I admit I spoiled her with my unconditional love. I chose her over everyone, but in the end, she chose everyone over me. There was an undercurrent that began to develop and, in the end, revealed that not only did she stop hearing me, but she rested every decision and action on what her children said and did. I understand that maybe we all just got caught up in those demonic devices of misconception and deception and incidences seem to confirm our perceptions. That is the devil and like a roaring lion he comes at unawares, like a thief in the night and catches us off-guard, when we least expect it and he kills Steals and destroys everything. He seeks whom he may devour. He seeks anyone who will let him use them. We all have free will and choice, but we wrestle not against flesh and blood (each other), but spiritual wickedness in high places.

Somebody got caught up in his grip. I have always been aware of his constant attacks on my life and my identity as I shared with you in Chapter 1. Subsequently, I had reservations about marrying my third wife because I did not want to unfairly subject her to my plight and pattern. I know Satan, for the most part because God taught us to" know your enemy", and in my gifts over the years, I've been able to discern and detect his character in operation. Because of the power of one and unquestionable faith in his word, I moved beyond that fear and chose not to allow him to deprive me of the support and inspiration that being with her afforded me. But in our dysfunctional family, there were a lot more spirits lingering in wait and targets for use. In the earlier stages of our separation, Our Bishop voiced his concern for reconciliation. At this point it seemed that the conclusion was inevitable. If I stay with my wife, I can't pastor a church. If I pastor a church, I can't stay with my wife. I was trapped into what I will call an inconclusive necessity. "I can't go, but I can't stay." Our philosophies, priorities and devotions are worlds apart. It was clear at this point that we could not carry out and reflect the quality and degree of leadership mandated by God's word as examples of kingdom living in the singular necessity of marriage in the two became one. Totally too many allowable interferences. The practiced priorities, devotion, ethics, moral and principled godly character that I exemplified, Was a hindrance to how they had chosen to live and What doctrine they chose to govern their lives. We were now totally not on the same page. We were butting heads and again A house divided against itself will not and had not prospered. How could I do what God required and reconcile or more over, what exactly is there to reconcile? The vows were violated. God first and forsaking all others. There is no change of hearts. No one acknowledges any wrongdoing. She and her children accept no responsibility for any aspect of our demise. I destroyed their family. I destroyed our church. I brought everything upon myself that caused me to suffer so deeply. She will not speak against, correct or oppose anything her children claim to be. A heart to do right by God, no matter what the cost and a family that won't budge from their ungodly disposition, how does it feel when trying to live Godly in an ungodly environment is unacceptable.

There was nothing to reconcile and now I feel that God's will in and for my life is defeated. I feel that I have failed God. The only way that I can fix what I messed up is to accept what I did not do and that has destroyed 50 years of my life. As I had warned, the Damage Done was now irreparable. I must conclude that I am but a mere mortal human being who does not have the power to transform the hearts of men. I Surrendered. I Let Go and I let God. On April 15th 2021, a judge in the family court of the District of Columbia, released me from God's Institution but my obligation and determination to glorify him still eats at my soul. How can the world undo what God has done? This gets deep and real if for Jesus you get deep and real. Satan is not playing with you. He is at all-out war with your faith in Christ. Whose report will you believe. As the head of my family, I accepted the blame as I have been doing for 50 years Almost in every situation, I've been in. In marriage, business and in church. I have taken the responsibility for all the wrongs everybody had done and said in my life.. Just like Christ did on the cross when he took all of our stuff upon himself, suffered and died. Did I fail God? And then I was reminded of God's word and Romans 12:18. He said," in as much as lieth in you to do, live peaceably with all men". Do as much as you can. Love as deeply as you can. Try as hard as you capably can. As Kenny Rogers would say" You've got to know when to hold them, know when to fold them. know when to pick them up and when to put them down." Ultimately, that is all that is required of you. Your life, your sanity and your God ordained fate depends on it.

In essence, give all that is within you to give, as I had advised my wife to do with her first husband. And ask yourself," Do I hold on and die, or let go and live? Do I hold on to what is clearly draining me of value and substance? When is enough, enough? When do I conclude that I can't handle or take anymore? When do I realize that I've given all that is in me all that I am required to give? And in response to all of these questions; Do I hold on knowing that the quality of life I desire to live is nowhere in sight, for the sake of fulfilling a promise to you. Do I hold on just to meet your expectation of me? Do I hold on because I promised to be there in spite of you cutting me till I bleed? Do I hold on because my vows said "till death do us part?

Because I had given all in the 15 year experience as a pastor, as I believed an agent of Christ should, and the 25 year experience as a husband, as a husband should, and that it all fell at the same time, I now faced starting all over again from scratch at the age of 66. I now face as I shared with you in the introduction the many aspects that affect our ability to hold on and die or let go and live. One of the major causes now, affected me, "starting all over again."

When the quality of life that God promised us in Genesis is depleting, deteriorating and Diminishing everything you touch: How long do I hold on to this hot coal or issue that's permanently scarring me and bringing me down?

When you hit rock bottom, do you hold on to the rock? NO! When you reach a dead end, you make a U-TURN

DO I HOLD ON AND DIE OR LET GO AND LIVE?   I CHOSE LIFE AND I'M FREE

HOLD AND DIE OR LET GO AND LIVE

Chapter 4

ENOUGH IS ENOUGH -IN AS MUCH AS LIETH IN YOU
Romans 12:8

I n Micah 6:8 God draws a clear and simple analogy as it pertains to life, relationships, business or personal regarding behavior and expectations. Even in our Christian walk and relationships with our creator, it says simply, "God has shown you o man what is good; and what does the Lord require of you, but to do justly, to love mercy, and to walk humbly with your God." In other words, only Justice, Mercy and humility. be straightforward, fair and honest and integrity will follow That pattern. A genuine Godly love for others will compel us to take this verse to Heart. There will be no desire or room for messing around with people, being underhanded, undermining, manipulative, self-seeking and playing games that result in a whole lot of unnecessary drama. I've also heard from Heaven that we should separate ourselves from among those who possess this character and attitude. Flee from the appearance of evil and refrain from gossiping, backbiting, judging and condemnation.

There you have it. Cut to the chase and the red tape, trim the fat (the high blood pressure elements of life). Stop the confusion and always making everything something that it's not. It's all ungodly and unacceptable behavior that results in nothing good. In any situation in life, we can ask the question, how much more am I obligated to withstand or endure that is not working in my best interest of good health and a sound mind and productivity. Life often entraps us in ties with people, expectations and responsibilities and sometimes brings us to a place where we just have no more to offer. Our efforts are in vain and for what? The accounts are empty, and everything is a struggle to overcome. There seems to be no way out and there's no viable reason insight to hold on to. As B.B. King would confer, " The Thrill Is Gone " .

A testament of these realities is often demonstrated in proverbial Expressions such as: I'm at the end of my road, or my wit's end. I can't take it no more or more popularly known, enough is enough. I found an answer worthy of sharing with you when you reached this level in life in Romans 12:18." In as much as lieth in you to do, live peaceably with all men". in as much as you can peacefully cohabitate in any capacity, it is required of you. As much as you are able to bear, give, love, understand, handle or relate, do so for it is required of you.

In all things give thanks. Even God realizes that it's hard to live with and love some people. Even God realized in his creation that we all have thresholds and indifferences, boundaries and tolerance levels. Find peace at all cost for in that is the essence of life and the peace of God that

passeth all understanding will keep your heart and mind through Christ Jesus, anywhere, at any time or with anybody. What a valuable commodity. There may be nothing wrong with you and truly there's nothing wrong with his creation, for he declared that even that was good. We were all created in His image and likeness and in every case, we're all just different.

Chapter 5
Business #1 & #2

Joyful Star Janitorial Cleaning Service was my first stab at being an entrepreneur. It started after my experience at Peoples Drug Store with the district manager who had me terminated because of his fear of being replaced. The threat he faced is that I would not be given such a prestigious position based on meeting EEOC guidelines but that my performance and quality of work earned and qualified me for the promotion. Joy and Star were the middle names of my two daughters. Starting out at 16 years old I wanted to be an example to my mother. But as I began to develop as a man, I obtained an inherent desire to leave a legacy to my children and live a successful life, and comfortable life. In this context I learned that if I was to succeed as an entrepreneur, my work ethic and determination would become essential components. It seemed in hindsight that what was also taking form was my spirit to give all that I could if I was to flourish. Working hard, working long and working smart were absolutely necessary and accomplishing anything I set my hand to. I developed the concept that as an entrepreneur, I had to produce. My theme was that if I don't work, I don't eat. There was no annual leave, sick leave or vacation pay to fall back on if sick. If I didn't work, I didn't eat. There was actually a time during my third marriage that because of the enormity of my responsibilities, if I missed work one day, something got turned off. So, I learned that I had to make things happen, not depend on my coworker or supervisor.

Joyful Star Cleaning Service was the first of four corporations that I set up. The going cost to set up a corporation I was told regularly was $5,000 and that by an attorney. So, as you can see, even from the beginning, I had to learn how to make it work from the very beginning to the end. Every facet of development. My greatest feat was eventually setting up a charitable 501c3 Corporation. I never had $5,000 to pay a professional, so I had to do it. It has always amazed me how we can perform when we're up against the wall or under pressure to produce. There was never a time that I entertained that I could not do something. As a matter of fact, my father used to tell me that I thought I could do anything. I did, and was confident that I could make it work. However, he would often inform me to leave that "God damn" electricity alone' because it would kill me". I believed him and I did.

I started Joyful Star Cleaning Service shortly after I lost my managerial job at Peoples Drug Store, which was immediately after my first wife informed me that she didn't need me anymore and asked me to leave our apartment. So, there I was in foreign territory again in my young life. No money. No job. Nowhere to live. A friend of mine, an Italian friend for 40 years until he died of COVID-19 often supported my infant daughter and son during my weekend visitation. If you can go through life and find just one true and devoted friend, you've experienced a miracle. He was that kind of friend. His confidence in me was unwavering and his constant support for me and my two children at that time was unconditional. He seemed to connect with me in recognizing ideas and potentially lucrative opportunities. Coming home one day I noticed a large piece of land that I thought would be perfect for a U-Haul location. When I arrived home and shared it with him, he responded, find out who owns it. The next day as I passed it there was a gigantic sign on the property that said, coming soon, U-Haul, and it's been a very prevalent and productive franchise for 40 years. Also, across the street from my first apartment there was a vacant lot that I thought would be perfect for a drive-through car wash. Although I dragged my feet on that one, consumed with divorce madness months later signs went up and one of the most popular car washes in Marlow Heights, Maryland, Sam's Car Wash now with multiple locations, was born. My head was always in the right place and I always knew that I had the potential of being a great contribution to society and not a detriment.

I needed to launch out on something that did not require a professional license because my education was limited, but my mind wasn't. A cleaning service is where I landed. I had heard a prediction at that time that by the end of 2020, service-oriented ventures would dominate the industry. Although I realize that you have to crawl before you walk or you have to start out small, I was convinced that this was not my processing. I've always thought big on a very large scale, why should I have to start at the bottom, I've already been there. Realities or otherwise, and God also has the ultimate call in that and all matters. However, I was fortunate enough at the start up stage to secure a contract cleaning $300,000 condos on New Mexico Avenue in Northwest Washington DC. An eloquent community with gold-framed foyer lighting and marble entrances. It was a new development and my job was to prepare them after construction for purchase. I was on my way and totally excited about the future success of this project and the image it afforded me. My best friend purchased all of the equipment and operating supplies that I needed for this huge project. With Extreme Caution, I hired 14 staff members to clean and laid out my goal and requirements for their performance. Even at that youthful and inexperienced age, I knew that proper preparation and quality work would land me a prosperous career. I had to and could make it happen.

As my life progressed, my friend assisted me in acquiring my first apartment in Carriage Hill in Marlow Heights, Maryland, right across from the car wash lot that I had envisioned. I would meet my staff on site each morning and return to my home to secure additional projects. Life was good. I was in control of my life and had adjusted from the loss of my first wife which resulted in high blood pressure and severe hair loss. We had only lived together for one year but remained legally married for four years. As a bachelor, I was visited one night by a friend who asked if she could take a shower. When she came out of the shower, wrapped in a towel, she mistakenly dropped the towel from around her body and sat on my burnt orange velvet dining room chairs. I forgave her and asked her to get dressed. No doubt, she was a sight to behold and thought that my request suggested that I had issues.

Truly, I did not, but my focus was on my success and not satisfying my fleshly desires. I was the captain of my fate, not her femininity. But God. And I was still married. During this time, my first wife expressed a desire to continue in our marriage and I honored her acknowledgement that our issues had stemmed mainly from her serious challenges and attitude in dealing with them. As our lives continued, the same problems began to surface and reoccur. One in particular was that she didn't think that it was fair that I was home all day and she had to go out and work. I've been told that if you have a weak marriage, don't go into business and if you have a weak business, don't get married. This concern was very disturbing for me. When she returned to me, I was self-employed, generating thousands of dollars monthly, paying a staff and totally supporting my lifestyle. I once asked her to go to the bank on Friday and compare her paycheck to my deposits for clarity and understanding. But the problem was not me and my negligence.

Her issues were still the psychological impact and trauma that she experienced from rape that still had not been therapeutically treated. And here I go again, a complete repeat of our destructive and painful separation. I had joined her as an equal participant in this Union that included two people accepting responsibility for our original demise. But I could not do it this time. I was building an empire, taking my child to daycare and sometimes her to work, satisfying all of my responsibilities and yet, it still was not enough. This time it got uglier. This time I was taken to court. This time I was handcuffed and taken to jail. And this time, I was on the verge of losing all that I had gained the first time when she put me out and all of my energy and enthusiasm was redirected. As if she had come back just to destroy me again when I should not be the one paying for the pain she experienced the years before we met. I love her. I knew she had been scarred deeply. It's in her behavior today. but in sympathy, marital commitment or obligation;

Do I hold on and die? It's destroying everything. Or let it go and live?

In the meantime. The quality of work by the Joyful Star Cleaning Service was depleting. My corporate image was diminishing before I could secure it. Developers were disappointed in the service I provided. There were Spots, dust, stains and debris in the condos when millionaires visited who had an interest to purchase. The performance of my staff was deteriorating. I was not given an opportunity to complete this huge task. My contract was rescinded. Dying before I could live. I never received any further work in that industry. A highlight in my life extinguished. In my journey at this significant crossroad I was preoccupied, consumed, overwhelmed and at a total loss. In this era of my life I tried to hold on, but it wasn't in my power to do. Control of my fate was in the hands of someone else and something else. The developer in my latest vision and the court system in my freedom. I didn't know what I was fighting or facing; love, marriage and children or an angel that came to rescue me.

You've got to know when to hold them, know when to fold them, know when to pick them up, and when to put them down. During my tenure in church, my third church, I had developed a theme or theory if you will. God has never given up on me, so I will never give up on anyone as a pastor. I applied that determination to my own life and chose to rise above those pitfalls and start all over again.

I remembered that during my military career I drove a 30,000-gallon fuel truck every day, so I chose driving in that it didn't require any professional credentials of which I didn't have. While I was considering some other deals, I needed a temporary project to keep me while I started researching that project. I just needed a temporary income for one year to get that project established. The taxi became the longest temporary job in history. For 38 years, it was flexible. I worked when I wanted to and most importantly, I was my own boss. It took care of me financially. It allowed me to be a blessing to others. It helped send five people to college and provided a one-on-one opportunity to minister directly to many as a Christian and later a minister about every conceivable issue you could imagine. McLaurin Taxicab Company. I rented a cab from the four largest companies in the District of Columbia for years until I decided that it was more advantageous to own my own car.

As I began to wrap my mind around this temporary business, I was reminded of the constant dream of something or somebody always working against me, pulling me down. Trying to soar, advance and rise up in life, but always confronted by some source, weakening, distracting and destroying my purpose at every turn. Arnold which means eagle, America's bird, lifting off but never able to develop a consistent Journey to fulfillment. This adventure may be different and that as a taxi cab driver, I had full control. Realizing once again that the only way things would get done is if I did them. I could not count on any outside resources. I drive. I get paid. The key was in managing my time efficiently. Because of its flexibility, it positioned me to pursue and conduct many tasks at my own pace simultaneously. To engage in Family Matters, Church projects, personal Endeavors and future aspirations, while maintaining a sufficient income. Multi-talented or multitasking.

You make the call.

In addition to totally managing our family of eight while my third wife was in college, its rewards were quite beneficial. Having my wife and three children in college, on occasion, three at one time, our income served a major role in how many scholarships or Grants we qualified for. As you can see, being self-employed and Reporting income or lack of income became a major juggling act. One year we lost $20,000 in scholarships and grants and my daughter asked me, what had I reported. I had reported making an additional $1,500 that year and lost $20,000 in grants. Go figure. I never repeated that problem again. McLaurin Taxicab became my ace in the hole. Realizing all that I envisioned, I knew I would always have this company as an ace in the hole when life's planned direction was interrupted. Clearly one of my wiser decisions in life and consistent resources even though it was not the most admirable choice of support. It was working and producing all of the essential elements of survival. Besides the money, the ministry was one of my greatest accomplishments in that car 10 to 14 hours a day and meeting people from every level of life.

However, there came a time when my ethics, Godly character and moral discipline behavior were tested. A passenger entered the front seat and did not inform me of her destination as I began to drive forward. After three blocks I asked her where she was going. She said I thought I would just ride around with you all day and I'll do whatever you want in the car for $4. A bit set back at her offer, I responded that out of all due respect ma'am I must decline your request. My first concern as a Christian man was that her life was at such a low point that she desired this remedy. As a man I submit that the thought was entertaining. Very entertaining actually. I thought about who I was. Where I was going and where I came from. My purpose is to present a life of substance and quality for my mother to see. My devotion to the work of Christ. Greater is he that is in me. This is somebody's daughter and all things done in the darkness shall one day come to light. What would my two little girls think? Just because we can't be seen, somebody is affected by every choice we make. Every word we speak and every act we commit.

Needless to say, after ministering to myself, I simply pulled over and respectfully asked her to leave my vehicle. I've always prided myself on providing for all a service fit for the president or my mama. In that I couldn't go wrong because of the high regard and respect I hold for both. I've always developed a safe and secure system of salvation and sustainability to keep me driven and focused on the vision and the mark that I was pressing toward.

The taxicab career accomplished all that it was divinely destined to accomplish. Provisions. Even though this one-year mission lasted for 38 years, it was the perfect lead-in for my third business, Joyful Star Child Development Center Inc. The question that I visited at the end of every era of my life since the age of 16 is do I hold on and die had now been converted and I could hold on to this venture and live.

My authority to drive remains. Maybe the trend is turning.

HOLD ON AND DIE OR LET GO AND LIVE

Chapter 5

Sermonic Lesson

YOUR GIFTS SHALL MAKE A WAY
Proverbs 18:16

There is a story in Matthews 25:15 that God uses to show us how he manages his kingdom. It's called a parable which is a heavenly story with an Earthly meaning. A man called together his servants and gave each one a gift, Talent or money that he felt they were capable of managing. Some had more than others but they were given these gifts based on their individual ability to manage them. They each had exactly what they needed to profit or succeed in life based on their place, purpose or pleasure in life. The answer that the master expected when he returned back home was what did you do with what I gave you? I gave you what I knew would not only produce a return in your life but also the resources to give back what you received. That could be called an attitude of gratitude. I must show appreciation to those who invest in my life. The two servants who received the two talents and five talents sowed, invested, nurtured, developed and put to use their talents or their gifts. The master was quite aware of their ability to make things happen with what they had received. But the servant who only had one talent, hid it in the ground, sat on it, complained and blamed the master who gave it to him. Who does that? I am not happy with what you gave me and so I am justifying why I did nothing with the blessing. Who does that? We are blessed by God to be a blessing to others. When you sit on your blessing, they produce no fruit and slowly wither away.

Your life is a gift from God. What you do with it is a gift to God. God wants you to use what you got to get what you want. After all, he gave it to you. The one talent was taken away and given to someone who would put it to good use. If you are not willing to drive the car, then give me the keys. How about that? Using what you have, as little as it may seem to be, helps build the kingdom and enhances the quality of your lives. When I married my third wife, I knew immediately that her youngest daughter's sincere aspirations were to be an actress and we nurtured that gift to adulthood.

Oprah Winfrey says that success is when preparation meets opportunity. That story speaks for itself. In spite of the innumerable obstacles in life, God does not want you to hide, hold or hoard your gifts and talents. He wants you to reap a harvest from them and if you do, they will surely make a way for you and all who are connected to you. The story clearly implies that you received what you received for two reasons at minimum. To live an Abundant Life and to enhance the kingdom of God on earth.

Your ability to perform a task or identify a talent may have been recognized in high school, college, on a family trip, in an accident or a painful experience where you hid it. We all have gifts and talents. To believe any part of God is to believe all of God. Rise up, reflect and re-examine your life. you just might be sitting on your blessing

Chapter 6
Business #3
1983-1988

I have always been encapsulated by an energetic force to thrive, accomplish and rise above circumstances. The eagle persona attached to my name, always trying to rise above where I am and soar. To live, to be, to fulfill that deep internal mission that I started out on. Driving down Georgia Avenue in Washington D. C., my love and compassion for children began to surface. I had begun a campaign to collect 50,000 signatures to support a platform to present to the mayor. Abusive acts towards children were dominating the news. The city's challenge to regulate the more than 600 Child Care Homes and centers were prevalent. Safety and quality care in daycare centers were at an all-time low. There were no laws on the books for illegal acts to a minor child. There was only a maximum charge if found guilty of an act toward a minor child and it was 10 years. Daycare center licenses were being issued under the table and physical inspections annually we're not being executed. I was working on Georgia Avenue one day in my taxi and I noticed a vacant building at 5123 Georgia Avenue, and it sparked a nerve. Three-story building was for rent for $1,500 per month. I did not have $3,000 to execute the lease but I had my best friend for 40 years willing to advance me all set up costs for a Child Development Center.

Upon inspection of the property I became aware that the prostitution and drug infested activity had been raided by the law and their business practices dissembled. I was excited and on fire at the opportunity to build this center. It was in the exact condition it was in on the night of the shutdown. Nothing had changed. I accepted it as it was. My work was cut out for me. I did all of the work, with the exception of major construction or electrical and plumbing requirements. If I was not working or on a church project, I was in that center from 4 a.m. to sometimes well into the midnight hour. As it was in everything I was involved in, I was totally immersed in this vision. I was 27 years old, single and about to make my mark on the universe.

My vision was to establish five childcare centers in the metropolitan area. I wanted to provide safe quality care at affordable prices, and I felt that the larger the volume of clients the lower the cost. The going rate at that time was between $80 and $120 per week and rapidly increasing. I charged $55 for the same quality and care as my competitors. I had an open-door policy which allowed my parents to visit without notice at any time that we were open from 6 a.m. to 6:30 p.m. I had a staff of 14 which freed me from any direct care of the children. The campaign for 50,000 signatures and a suggested list of infractions was still active. I lost my contractor in the middle of preparation because I wouldn't allow him equal partnership. Issues with my landlord arose also because I wouldn't allow him equal partnership. As it usually was, somebody was always trying to capitalize on my ideas, my heart and my potential to elevate them. Use me. I was young, very limited in resources and he used this as leverage to pressure and persuade me to partner with him. That did not work. My rent was due on the first day of the month. If it was not paid, I had an eviction notice posted on my door on the second day to go to court on the third. Pressure. That's the process that he used to coerce and manipulate me into giving him 50 percent of my vision. Somehow by court date I was able to accumulate the full rent. This was my challenge each month with not enough clientele to pay all of my expenses yet. One day I was not able to pay by the court date. I left to go to court realizing that I had run out of steam. I was defeated. When I returned this time, it would be with the news that I had lost the case, and my dream. In court that morning when our case was called, I answered present. When my landlord's name was called, there was no answer. The judge hit his gavel on his desk and said, "case dismissed". This is one of those times when I realized that long before I met and accepted Jesus, he had been with me all the time. As I drove back to the center with tears rolling down my face, the O'Neal twins began to sing on my radio:

I was guilty of all the charges,

Doomed and disgraced.

But Jesus with his special love,

Saved me by his Grace.

He pleaded, and he pleaded, and he pleaded my case,

And I'm so glad that Jesus dropped the charges, and now I'm saved by his grace.

I was guilty for oh so long.

Lived in sin too long.

But Jesus, with his special love,

Reached out with his arms so strong

He picked me up and turned me around

Gave me a brand-new song

Jesus dropped the charges

And now to him I belong.

And to this day, that is why I love him so, and he's so real to me.

Somehow, someway, somewhere, someday---- he will deliver on time.

I now had the opportunity with one clean sweep to show my mother who she was through my success and how everything I touched at church and at work was flourishing.

Originally, I had only leased the basement and the first floor but now I had reached capacity with a waiting list of 30 children. So, I rented the top floor and it was filled to capacity. I was bringing business into the neighborhood. Stores around me were flourishing. The image of the whorehouse had completely dissipated. In the next block, a hardware store had decided to relinquish his two corner buildings and relocate to Maryland. Because of our image and success. He offered me both leases. He was as he stated, impressed by my success. One was to be an infant care center and the second was to be a bookstore, carrying religious books, daycare supplies and teaching aids. This was all at my disposal now and my reputation as a young entrepreneur was escalating.

The state of professional care and rising child abuse incidents were fueling my concerns simultaneously even though I was progressing at a rapid pace. I had almost 100 children, an infant care center and a store. The children loved me and lived to see me every day. My genuine care and love for them was natural. It was indeed a gift from God.

Unfortunately, staff and parents were beginning to draw to me also. Most of my staff were single and 80 percent of my clientele was single, some with two or three children. Single, godly, and successful had now made me a target, a good catch. Potential and availability was now dominating my space and being approached was an uninvited constant distraction. My total focus was on providing the best care that our children deserved and needed and they were consistently searching for a viable partner and lover. I was sincerely in a war zone. Distracted beyond desire or the ability to manage respectfully without the perils of rejection. I was being waited for after closing, pulled to the side, and snatched into corners. Children were being used as pawns to entrap me. Set me up. I was a player by force and not by choice, constantly explaining why I must stay focused on tasks and that was my vision. I was propositioned by a single mother who had three children. She literally handed me a written contract one day establishing me as her slave master if I would just take her and her children under my direct personal care. I have to admit, Lord have mercy, that she was as pretty and fine as they come. She approached me one day pregnant with a fourth child, realizing that it was just not intelligent or feasible to have this child, and she needed $300 for an abortion. I am still apologizing to God for doing so but I just couldn't fathom her birthing another child who would be deprived as the three that she had, whom I was also discounting childcare fees. I was totally into my work and heartfelt desire to fix everything and I was too close for comfort. What a painful and long-term lesson to learn, even though I repeated it later. I allowed her to use the school van to this procedure while her children remained at the center. No one knew what I was doing. I was standing outside as I often did, greeting parents when she returned. She was drained, weak, leaning and about to collapse and wreck the vehicle. Imagine a young preacher living with that scene and the possible liability.

Those Infamous words were spoken to me one day," if I can't have you, no one else will". That, if I had known how it would play out, was frightening, to say the least. While being stretched, pulled and propositioned were ever increasing God was continuing to establish our name and increasingly provide all of the resources that we needed to expand. In the midst of the great balance and challenge that we faced; I recall a little girl. In the morning as I would stand out front greeting parents, a parent would get off the Metro bus at the end of the block, see her daughter across the street knowing that I had my eyes on her and she would return to the bus. Once crossing the street and setting her eyes on me, she would start running as fast as she could the entire block and then as I kneeled down she would leap up into my arms. I was so afraid one day that I was not going to catch her. The admiration I shared with a four year old and the unquestionable trust that she had that I would catch and embrace her as she entered School. Truly an awesome and inspirational scene to watch. She kept running and I kept catching.

I continued to manage my vision as physically and emotionally consuming as it was. It's value now had reached $1.2 million. Energized by the success story that I had so desperately envisioned, I was totally motivated until April 8, 1988. There was a news flash. "Breaking news, a preacher in a daycare on Georgia Avenue abuses children. Details at 4". That, straight out of left field, unexpected and shattering headline was me. I literally had no idea or anticipation of an accusation of such magnitude. My daughter watched that evening on TV and asked her mother, my first wife., 'Do you think Daddy did that?" She responded, "It's possible." My first wife, who was raped, answer caused my daughter to need therapy. I was now in suspended animation and waiting to see the news story. The story alleged that I stuck a ruler in a little girl's vagina. I had two little boys put their penises together in a bathroom stall that had three feet high swinging doors, any adult was able to see even from a distance in a huge open space. Other parents began to make stunning accusations. You may find it completely surprising that the accusations and continued stories developing were from every parent that I had respectfully rejected their request to have a relationship. I had learned over the years of the devastation that a scorned woman can cause. True or false, here I was. Every woman who I had not obliged, disappointed, was engaging in their 15 minutes of fame and at the expense of a young, single, thriving preacher.

Just as that one sexual encounter of my third wife's daughter destroyed a 15-year church and a 25-year marriage. Just as that one act of rape that my first wife experienced, destroyed my marriage, my passport rejected and my credit. This one lie was now destroying a $1.2 million dream. Over time, all of the accusations and claims fizzled out and were dismissed with one exception. Of course, by now I was destroyed.

May I interject or impose a question to you, the reader?

How many relationships with church, friends, neighbors, marriages, co-workers or family have been ugly and devastated because of jealousy, Envy, Vengeance and rage?

First to thine own self be true. The answers could be quite alarming. The only remaining accusation and claim put me on trial for eight days at a cost of $100, 000 and in a civil lawsuit for $36 million. It involved a four-year-old little girl whom I had never been around alone. She had only been enrolled in my daycare for four days. Hospital records at Children's Hospital in Washington DC indicated that she had been seriously violated before that four-day enrollment and further abused after the four-day enrollment. Severe abuse they stated.

The city was under media pressure. The investigator was seeking a promotion. The cameraman from Channel 9 who had illegally seized photos was immediately relocated out of the area. No one wanted the truth. Everyone wanted a story. Records indicated that the little four-year-old girl lived in a crack house. In her medical records at Children's Hospital, the mother recorded that she blamed the child's father for committing these acts against his child. I have a recording from the family that was ruled inadmissible blaming the father. The father owed drug dealers thousands of dollars and set me up and my Center to pay this debt. The State's Attorney chose not to press charges against me, and in the civil suit, the court and a jury of 12 found that the acts against this minor child were not caused by me nor did they occur at my facility. But the damage had been done. A life shattered. A vision destroyed. And no one ever heard how the story ended.

Think about the unbearable consequences you can cause others the next time you choose to tell a little lie. The Bible says that the day would come when it will be easier to believe a lie than to accept the truth. Who searches for the truth? No one wants to hear the truth? until they become the subject of a lie. The good book also States that they shall know the truth and the truth shall make them free. In interpretation, that truth must be that Jesus is Lord of Lord and to the utmost He saves. He will pick you up and turn you around. Hallelujah, Jesus does save.

A dream that had engulfed my spirit and gift from God since I was 12 years old was fulfilled and destroyed by one lie and one doctored news story. The Devil comes like a thief in the night, to catch you off-guard, set you up to kill, steal and destroy the work of Christ and good in your life. No one affected by that major news article ever heard from me or about me publicly again. Maybe the media should reverse their practices, follow up and inform the nation of good, justice and positive results. It's called restoration. To a degree, and with some small effort, we all have the power to fix what we break. As we do, the power to break. The icing on the cake was that my attorneys strongly advised me to stay away from children because this stigma and shame would haunt me for the rest of my life. Isn't that advice devastating of itself, to knock me down and then tell me I must stay there. Thank God for the cross.

Before my second wife decided to marry me because of the subsequent remedy I sought from the city, I was totally alone. When my second wife came, she actually brought a vividly clear replica for me to envision. The audacity of the Devil who will stoop to any level to castrate, annihilate and devastate the children of God. And I sped home every night to be with him (my wife) because he was all I had left. On the floor. Burning to death. Drowning. Losing my mind all alone. I considered suicide twice. I had Heineken beer bottles around and throughout my apartment like dominoes. I don't like beer. I couldn't sleep for 30 days so I was trying to drink myself drunk so that I could fall asleep. The more I drank, the keener and awake I became. I could not drive my taxi after three days for security reasons, so I tried to drink myself to sleep. The devil had me. I was in a vacuum and at a point of no return. How could I face the world again? I recalled that I had been seeking 50,000 signatures to enact legislation to protect our children and now I had become subject to them. Planned or unplanned? Strategically orchestrated by the powers to be to shut me down before I exposed them?

And so, here I was again, trying to soar, climb and grow, rise up, and a lie, an accusation, strategic, circumstantial or accidental. I don't know, But I was down, failed with nothing and no one to fight for or with me. There was my brother of course. My family had arrived in Washington in 1964 and my brother grew up in the drug, gangster/ hustle mentality. His theme was always centered around the survival of the fittest. He had five families, drove the best cars and lived lavishly. He had made me an offer around this time. In order to launder thousands of dollars, he would completely Finance all five Child Care Centers. However, I could not engage him in his offer because of the extreme differences in our lifestyles. I was simply doing Jesus and He wasn't. He was very angry at my loss and treatment and he offered to help me in one of the few ways that gangsters and hustlers handle people hurt people or offend them. It's called annihilation. One day he asked me to give him the addresses of anyone and everyone that was causing or contributing to my problem. When I say that I was hurting, I mean that I would have done anything to relinquish what I was going through. Being fully aware of his remedy and intent, I said there's wives and innocent children at those addresses. He responded that that was their problem and not ours. While I entertained his request for about 45 seconds, my conscious eliminated the thought of seeing all of those houses on fire or bodies on the ground, while he laid comfortably on the beach in another country. But make no mistake, I was hurting and at my lowest. That lifestyle had never been my choice and because of Jesus and my genuine love for his children, it was not about to entertain me now even at the depths of my suffering. I remember Jesus being taunted with "if you can save yourself, come down off that cross". The words of the song writer brought clarity even to my series of issues. He would not come down from that cross to save himself, he decided to die just to save me.

My brother was shot and killed on New Year's Eve of that year. He was very angry at me for not letting him help me. His way. My grandmother in North Carolina also died two days later but we could not bury either one of them. Because my brother was the tenth of 10 homicides and all homicides had to be autopsied. We could not leave to bury my grandmother until we were finished with him. Two corpses and we couldn't touch either.

I felt like Mahalia Jackson who sang, "My soul look back and wonder how did I make it over".

I was very angry with God, when my family asked me to come to North Carolina and preach at our annual family reunion. I truly had nothing to say to God, about God and truly not for God. I had tried so hard to live the life he requested of me since I had met him in 1980. I was working in a church and in some 10 to 12 different Ministries or projects and I was giving all I had to become a good and productive asset to society. He was God. He had control. He could stop anything he wanted. He could start anything he wanted. I trusted him. For some reason he chose not to stop me from suffering, but to allow me to go through that turbulent storm. I would not curse him like Job was requested but I had nothing to say on his behalf. I went to North Carolina for our weekend of activities, realizing that on that Sunday morning they were expecting me to stand in a church and preach God's word. Unprepared and unwilling, what in the world was I going to say? I wish I would. I did. I was introduced around 11 that morning and when I stood at the podium I said, my subject this morning is, "Peace in the midst of the storm". I've been told for decades that that 8 Minute sermon was the shortest and most powerful word of inspiration that I've ever spoken. I don't know where it came from and I don't even know what I said, but whatever it was, they heard it, received it and never forgot it." straight out of heaven" I suppose.

I returned to Washington, still fully engaged in this battle. When you hear that," it can't get any lower", Don't believe it. When you hear of

Murphy's Law, "if it's possible for something to go wrong, it will." Believe it. There was no one in my universe that had not been adversely affected by my situation. All I had left in life was church (that's scary). My church, where I had been for twenty years, abandoned me. When I arrived there in 1980, after the breakup of my first wife (I don't need you) I had an Infant child in a bassinet and a two-year-old attached to my hip. I worked hard there. I grew there. I loved there. I learned there. I built Ministries there. But as soon as they saw me plastered on the evening news, they immediately abandoned, disowned and treated me like filth. Never once asking me if I was okay. Did I need help? Was I innocent or guilty? Not even the pastor. The man of God. The Angel of God's Church sent from Heaven. I suppose it was partly that experience that strongly compelled me to love like Jesus and not like man. Give like Jesus and not like man. Sacrifice like Jesus and not like man. Because man will leave you disappointed at the Midnight Hour of your life.

I had to go to church. Not mine. It was all I had left. So I went to a church. As pissed off as I was with Jesus, I had to go because my life was still in his hands. I would wear sunglasses, arrive very late and sit in the back so nobody would see me. Leave before the benediction so no one would notice or approach me. That Pastor soon found out who I was and befriended me. He offered to invite and allow me to participate as a member and preacher. Bold and courageous he was. I've often referred to him as the biggest little man I know. However; in all good conscious, I could not and would not subject him to the public ridicule, slander, and humiliation that I was enduring. So, I'll live with the damage, the great loss and suffering I endured, but I will not live without the love of Jesus in my heart.

I Let Go. For if God be for me, he is more than the whole world against me.

I was fighting with all that was in me, to restore my integrity and to protect my image, to save my business. I didn't really know who I was fighting. The city, the parents, the teachers, or the law. Who was the main source of my detriment?

VENGEANCE, ENVY, JEALOUSLY, RAGE

What am I fighting? I was spending money I didn't have. The more I tried to hold on, the more I was losing my grip. How long, Lord? How much do I have to endure ?It is killing me. Literally draining the very life from me. The very quality and substance of my life has diminished. I have no control. Do I hold on and die? Or let go and live?

The choice really wasn't mine anymore to make. Maybe therein is the answer. When you have no vested influence, no voice or choice in the outcome of a situation. Now would be a good time to give it to someone who does. Now would be a good time to decide whether to:

HOLD ON AND DIE OR LET GO AND LIVE

Chapter 6

PEACE IN THE MIDST OF THE STORM
Mark 4:35-41

In 1988 I found myself in the midst of fulfilling the dream of a lifetime as I was rapidly establishing a chain of Child Development Centers in Washington D.C. My business was valued at one point two million dollars and I was totally immersed in and inspired by the great work that I was doing for God in my first church. And then, all of a sudden, literally in less than five minutes, the bottom fell out of my ship and I began to drown. Life has a way of Shifting directions at the drop of a dime. As a result, my life was shattered, I contemplated suicide twice, lost my business, was publicly humiliated, my church of eight years disowned and rejected me.

I faced $36 million in lawsuits and 40 years in prison. During this process I found only one place of consolation. It was alone in a park in Adelphi Maryland where a constant stream of water flowed. As I set there on a rock one day, I observed that at one place in that stream the waters came rushing down and angrily splashing and beating against the rocks and fallen tree. Gushing rapidly and then just a few feet away the water was still and calm. I thought as I sat there in an unimaginable world that this is the essence of life.

One day life is good and things are going so well and suddenly life's raging storms like in the story of The Three Little Pigs, comes huffing and puffing and blowing your house down. My storm was at the least rugged, raging, tumultuous and turbulent and knocking down everything I had worked so hard to build. I was 27 years old. Respect, dignity, integrity, reputation and a sense of overwhelming accomplishments were all lost in five minutes.

It reminded me of the story in Mark. The disciples were on the ship one day and Jesus was downstairs sleeping and resting. A great storm arose and the wind and waves began to beat up against the ship till it was almost filled with water. They ran downstairs, woke him up and said, master don't you care that we are about to die. " He woke up wondering why they were panicking so and asked them," where is your faith?" You've walked with me and watched me heal and perform all kinds of Miracles for weeks. And he spoke to the storm and said," peace be still and there was calm". If you go into the storms of life with Jesus in your heart, by your side or on your ship, you can come out unscathed because the battle is really not yours, it's the Lords. He will not allow you to go through more than you can bear. Just knowing that he's there will give you peace in the midst of your storm, if you just don't panic. I am also reminded, that we should be not weary in well doing, for in due season, the appropriate season, we will reap if we just don't panic. The songwriter summarized that story with these words.

Master the tempest is raging, the billows are tossing high

The sky is overshadowed with darkness, no shelter or help is nigh.

Carest thou not that we perish? How canst thou lie asleep?

When each moment so madly is threatening, a grave in the angry deep.

Whether the wrath or the storm-tossed sea, or demons or men or whatever it be.

No water can swallow the ship where lies,

The master of ocean and Earth and skies.

They all shall sweetly obey my will. Peace, peace be still.

Chapter 7
My First Church
1980-2000

I have felt like I've been working against an invisible force to stop, distort, or destroy everything I start to believe in, imagine, attempt to accomplish, or fulfill anything that I touch. Tear down everything I desired to build. An enemy built into my path to circumvent or cut me off at every turn. What a way to live. But it's happening. The enemy, IN-A-ME or attempting to be, to shut down at will my path to Life, Liberty and the Pursuit of Happiness. To date, he has always successfully concocted some scheme or remedy to perpetuate that end, and convince, twist and deceive the minds of all players he chooses to use. What an internally interwoven plot and battle I've fought and couldn't see but knew it was there seizing the moment. Often seeing it in the development but never able to escape its agenda. It has become very hard for me to blame or find fault with those he uses to perfect his demonic will. I can't hate anyone. While I can't live with his victims anymore. The Bible says love your enemies. I find myself loving them and understanding them in spite of their inability to detect his agenda when it's clear and their weak resistance to oppose his power over them. There is much proof to the statement, the devil made me do it. And one day he chose to literally give me a glimpse of his appearance. He used a beautiful, gifted and talented young woman filled with the love, and knowledge of Christ and his word. A perfect description of what I asked God for in a mate. A swollen image of ET, the Extra-Terrestrial with muscles IN his face of different colors and in my bed that I yearned to be with, in my state of utter humiliation. Check the web for clarification. How do I live with these constant phenomena knowing that in all matters pertaining to me, it's just a matter of time before it starts formulating its attacks?

However, I get up every day after each failed Adventure, searching for that opportunity or hope that like Job, God says to him enough is enough. Take your hands off of him. You do not have any authority to take his life. I submit to you that Hepatitis C in my body for 44 years didn't kill me, couldn't kill me, double and walking pneumonia, a heart murmur, chronic kidney disease, diabetes, an enlarged prostate, cirrhosis of the liver, sciatica, blocked arteries, high blood pressure, or an almost punctured heart, couldn't kill me. Science and medicine say that they're all in me working on me but seemingly God is saying, "so am I".

And then he shows up in church, the body of Christ and the household of faith. In December of 1980, in the cold of the winter,

sleeping in my car after my first wife asked me to leave, this pattern of my life or phenomena started all over again. There are times when the depth and power of a mother's love can't resolve the magnitude of her children's issues. I shared with my mother the issues involving my first wife's dilemma with the rape and the how upon conception, she concluded that she didn't need me anymore. My pain and my frustration. I remember her saying so confidently and clearly, "son I can't help you. you need Jesus." And who is that I thought. She said, you need to go to church, implying that that place is where I would find all of the answers that I needed. The following Sunday I was in service and was there for the next 20 years. During the first ten years, I may have missed service five times. My first lesson for life was that God so loved the world that he gave (all he had), his only begotten son. And that his son Jesus loved us so much that he suffered and died the most excruciating and painful death in Roman history. The fact that someone could love me so much that he was willing to die so that I could live, that was my takeaway. That was my cut card, that was the game changer for me. The Cross sold me. The cross represented pain and suffering for someone else. I had just given all that I had to my first wife for one year and was now suffering for what somebody else did. I connected. I was sold out. My heart became fixated on his mission (unconditional love), and my life on his suffering. When I say for God I'll live and for God I'll die, it is with honor, gratitude and determination no matter how much it cost me.

If he was willing to die for me, then I am willing to live for him. While not understood by many who don't possess these convictions, I opened my heart for what would become ongoing attacks on my character and a target for abuse. Caring for God's people, in spite of their issues and shortcomings the way he cared for me, became fixated in my heart. it became my reason for living and it started with the appreciation for my mama at age 16 and my love for children at age 12. A real-life replica of who he was and how he rolled. When I arrived there, I was separated. I had one child clinging to my leg at two years old and another in a bassinet on my arm around four months of age. The pattern became based on what my duties were on that Sunday.

One person would grab the bassinet, and another would grab the two-year-old as I proceeded to do ministry. It was awesome to behold, how they immediately embraced me during that painful transition from my failed marriage. I was losing my hair and my blood pressure was off the hook and has been since. I got very busy right from the start. The Pastor and founder asked me to build him a Sunday School. How was I to build or teach about something I knew nothing about? The very day that he asked me, he said I will help you. One day during the following week, his wife gave him dinner and when she took his utensils to the kitchen, he slumped over and died. All on my own now trying to carry out the vision of another man. I often thought when I arrived in heaven, I would inquire of him," how do you ask someone to help you and then you roll out."? It was a challenging task and I disliked a dead man for a while for setting me up. The ministry grew and so did my involvement in other countless duties; Director of Youth Ministries with 14 members on my team, Worship leader, male chorus, gospel chorus, quartet, Bible study and Sunday school teacher, lawn care, Transportation Ministry and custodian. When I wasn't at the Childcare Center. I was working on a church project. I was ultimately inspired to become a preacher and in so doing took on the responsibility of Pulpit assistance. Clearly my life as a

new Christian was now in full development. The church membership grew and there were many accomplishments attributed under my watch and work as a youth leader.

As time progressed there was a family who were founders of the church who began to regulate and totally control the official operation. The Pastor had died, and we were without a Shepherd for more than three years. It is never good for a church to operate too long without a pastor/spiritual leader. This order is mandated by biblical Doctrine. The church had become the possession of that selected family and their Close Associates, and not God's Institution for Kingdom building. It is operated at and regulated on the doctrine and principles Christ set forth to reflect his image, personage and eternal glory. And is led by one who is chosen by God's Holy Spirit. It is not man's Church. It is God's Church. Man is given the awesome privilege of managing the store if you will. We were far from this Spirit led and unified state of affairs. This family had seized total control and were dominating every aspect of this Godly establishment. It was literally declared one day by them that" this is our church". Our families church, my father's church. There came a time when a new pastor had been voted in according to the standard protocol and the guidelines that govern how a pastor is chosen. The head Deacon and father of this family rejected the decision of the church and recommended the man that he wanted. He then deceptively manipulated the church to officially select him.

Once in office he began immediately to dominate and control his leadership. The thirst and drive for power will always lead to corruption and destruction. As will the love of money (greed). It has not failed yet. Everywhere that I have gone in my 50 years, there have been elevated acts of jealousy, envy and a threat to my Effectiveness and popularity. Simple, down to earth, uneducated and genuine. Just doing all that I do for my mama, and the Glory of God.

Complaints, discord and ill will from members became widespread. Nothing felt right or fair. Fear to approach leaders and speak out about concerns was at the forefront. Dictatorship and not inclusivity were an often-expressed emotion. I just don't feel like I'm an important part of my church that I work so hard to be successful and everything is always secretive and hidden. My voice, input, ideas are never sought, or appreciated. Just do what you're asked. This was the cry. Because of my personality, ease to approach and genuine care for people, I was approached frequently. to reach out, ask questions. Say something. I'm reminded of the slogan that originated at the airport." see something say something". That posture at my first church became my demise. It tends to expose what people don't want you to see or know. Expectations of me were clear. Standing for their concerns and desires were there. It's always an immediate detection wherever I go. That's probably why my heart is under constant attack. I was so involved in so much that it was always easy to share and talk to me. I was sold out and so sincere about my relationship with Christ and his concerns for his people. Speaking out and inquiring was easy for me. Taking on the hurt and pains for others was a developing trend in my life, and like Christ, it has gotten me in a whole lot of trouble. Especially with people who don't share my genuine convictions as a Christian even though they walk by the same faith. I began to speak out, ask questions, not only because I cared but because others cared also only to receive major backlash, from the powers to be.

Their dislike for me was mounting as this new young pastor began his tenure and they began to impress upon him to quiet me. How many times have I entertained my stand as a Christian man? If I shut up, I have to account to God. If I speak up, I may be condemned by men. Well, my loyalties are as clear now as they were when I met Christ on the cross. For God I'll live and for God I'll die. The inference being placed on me now was, I was a troublemaker. I needed to mind my own business, stay in my lane and be removed from all of the offices that I held. All of the limitations and boundaries that God never put on us. I was becoming radical in my behavior and searching for truth and Justice in God's house. I was taught that we were many members, but we were one body, on one accord, walking by the same faith. My stand and my personality was causing pressure on those who were equally concerned as I was but scared or too weak to fight. My ecclesiastical Bond and relationship with the Pastor had become very challenging and was creating a wedge between him and his leaders. That was clearly a no-win for me. He had begun the process of licensing me to preach, but under pressure refused to provide me a physical license as if to imply its leverage.

It was clearly evident the order and quality of Christian living in the body (Church) was not being exemplified. There was confusion, corruption, disrespect, unfairness, insensitivity, emotional instability and a blatant misrepresentation of the Kingdom living principles that Christ established on Earth. And I spoke concern to these issues, not as I saw them but as God ordained them. I had come to this place where God salvages damaged and broken spirits like he did mine. This place where his love and his word restored and redeemed me from the curse. This place where I had learned so much and grown tremendously in statue, character, fatherhood and unconditional love. But here I was on the verge of collapse, accused of stealing, lied on, integrity questioned, labeled a troublemaker, rejected and all of my good works cut off and discredited.

And Satan, once again, had me positioned for an insurmountable attack. And on April 8, 1988 that unseen and unpredictable explosion came in the form of," breaking news, "Preacher in a daycare on Georgia Avenue abuses children." This is an approach or a psychology networks used to Grasp your interest and attention. I guess it's called ratings. It's presented as a statement of fact to get you there, capture your sensitivity to an issue, intensify the story to lure you and then introduce it as a possibility. A preacher in a daycare abused children. The power of word formation. State a fact and then in the story transform it into a simple allegation. A gigantic network organization gives you an absolute to draw you and once you are there simply states what somebody said. Because of the sensitivity of the matter, the damage is done before you even hear the details. How many lives have been destroyed for nothing? Once the concept sets in your mind for hours you begin to entertain the severity, despicability, disdain and sorrow for the victim who you don't even know has been victimized or not. And by the time you actually hear the story there's an already formulated conclusion based on human compassion. The advanced thought permeates the mental capacity, and then anticipates the supporting facts. Anticipates that reality that it really doesn't require much more to confirm the fact. Prejudgment, at its most dangerous level without accountability. The headline presents a sound, secure and convincing thought and the term" breaking news" draws the "oh my God" tone. Why would somebody do that? To capture the targeted audience. Dropping the word allege in the story after pounding the act and its heart-wrenching trigger becomes of little significance. The damage to one's career is actually done before the article airs, it just attaches a name.

The story aired on Friday, April 8,1988 at 4 p.m. and on Sunday morning, April 10th the church rejected my very existence. Godly leaders, deacons, pastors, preachers and members that I worshipped and worked with in church for eight years and in 45 hours acted like I wasn't even there. Just that fast my family of Christian friends disowned me. To this day 33 years later not one of them has asked how are you? Do you need anything? Are you innocent? God's going to work it out. I'm praying for you. They immediately judged and condemned me to hell. And we wonder why the church has lost its power to save the world. Fear of associating with who the world says is bad has crippled us. Even though, we have all sinned and come short of the glory of God and even while we all were yet sinning, Christ died for all of us anyhow. How easy it was for Christians to join the world in attacking one of God's Own Elect. JUST FOR YOUR THOUGHTS.

I was simply guilty as factually stated until proven innocent in that headline. The channel never returned publicly with the pronounced verdict, not guilty. No one ever inquired. The church and its leaders actually judged and condemned me more than the world. How real is this to us? There can be nothing worse or more dangerous than surface religion. The church is Christ in living color and full operation on Earth. The church is Jesus. Psalm 139 Chapter 7 said, if you ascend into heaven and make your bed in hell, I'll be there with you. Will never leave you or forsake you. The church turned their back on me, and left me for dead.

If the church represents Christ, then did Christ leave me? That Sunday after the article aired and for all of the subsequent years that followed, God's church rejected the work and will of Christ in my life and simply chose the safe and easy way out. Whose report will you believe? How many people have you left disappointed in the midnight of their life? They didn't even express a concern. How did it go? Did things work out for you, whom I told last week" I love you".

I'm reminded of the time when Jesus was facing the most difficult time in his ministry. They were hunting him down to crucify him, and they asked the Apostle Peter, didn't you know Jesus? Didn't you follow Jesus? Peter responded in parallel, I don't know him. I didn't hang out with him, and I have no recollection of what you are talking about. When he needed him the most, he acted like he didn't even exist. What a sad state that the churches of God are still leaving God's chosen in their hour of despair. What purpose do we serve God, the kingdom or your friend when you can't be there when they need you the most because you exemplify the story of the Samaritan who everybody that walked by Justified why they should just keep moving and not lend a helping hand. How far have we come? Or have we even really started?

These are the reasons why the work of Christ has consumed me, through my own experience and they are why I am choosing to share them with you. To me, it's so wonderful to know that Jesus is mine. I vowed as a pastor, never to give up on anybody, never abandon people in their darkest hour and never allow the world or its opposers to influence the unconditional love that I have for my brother or any of God's children.

In the minds of family, friends, church and society, the position I found myself in was guilty until proven innocent. And once I was proven innocent, the thought of me had faded into, "well I guess he got what was coming to him". There must have been some truth to it because nothing more has been said. To this day, as the lawyer instructed me, people are still hating on me and they still don't know the truth and 33 years later, they still won't even ask me.

After this incident, I remained a member of my church for 12 years. I was stripped of all of my duties and titles. For the last two years of my tenure there, I was literally called the devil, openly, publicly and from the pulpit, the holiest and most honorable desk there is. I was accused and blamed for every problem, Challenge and pressure that the church was experiencing even before the incident. We have to stand tall and together I would hear from church leaders, because the devil is trying to destroy us and then they would focus their attention on me. They just wanted me out. My third wife now and family were suffering persecution and rejection because of me. My mother and father were experiencing humiliation and degradation because of me. They were both deacons and were expected to exhibit the same disdain others were projecting against me. My pain was elevated one day when my father concluded Under pressure that I must be guilty because otherwise the media and subsequent stories wouldn't have said it. A knife, sharp knife, penetrating slowly into my flesh. That's what it felt like. I could not sleep. I could not work. The quality of life that I had chosen to live in Christ eight years earlier in that same place was now depleting and rapidly diminishing my desire to live.

My mother, who I left home at sixteen to show her the value and appreciation for her sacrifices, was in church, now every Sunday morning watching her son fighting for his life while his friends and loved ones abandoned him at every turn. Kept a safe distance from me. Like Mary ,standing at the foot of her son's cross, utterly humiliated and beat to a pulp. Suffering for everybody when he could have come down and lived a life of value and substance. How dare me, to compare my cross to my Savior's cross. I assert to you that on different levels, we all have crosses to bear. Hurting like hell, I was standing in church and out of church. I was fighting to do the right thing. To clear my name and restore my integrity. I would never give up. I would never accept defeat. I was in too deep.

Shockingly, there was absolutely no concern or compassion for my unbearable circumstances from my church. A body of redeemed souls. They had not only publicly attacked me, but I was always under scrutiny. They had removed me from all leadership roles a second time and any association with any of the works that I had done so consistently and successfully during my tenure. The way that I was being treated was outrageous and without regard for my person, decency or respect. Inhumane. I had a right to be there and I had a right to serve. The unorthodox, technical and complex personality that had been prophesied over my life emerged. I sued the leadership for their treatment and accusations against me, and I sued the Pastor who tolerated and allowed it to happen without correction and his blatant disregard for my right to live and dwell in that Society.

They hired an attorney and flipped the switch and twisted my intent and purpose. In doing so, they now added to the accusations against me that I was in violation of God's word that states that we should not take the church of God to court. They embellished this perpetrated Context on the minds of the members Sunday after Sunday in order to further cause friction, discord and disconnect between them and I. Pure evil deeply permeated and programmed in God's Church. They publicly pounded on the membership, how despicable I was for suing the church, the God that I had claimed I loved so much. The Church as an organization governed by rules indoctrinated in its bylaws was not sued. Those whose responsibility it was to uphold those guidelines were being held accountable for failing to do so. They had to be held accountable for not only hurting my person without conscious, but they also hurt others. They used others as prey and crushed their spirits in doing so. I needed for them to know that in God's eyes and the constitution of the United States, they did not have a right to do that. To escape their own acts and plots to control and deceive, they used this scheme to twist my intent, to shift and cover up their unfair, unequal treatment. Their favoritism and control tactics were to empower their family and Inner Circle. They condemned me to cover their wrong.

The judge, while she voiced clear reservation in church versus State matters, was compelled to consider the degree of treatment against a citizen of the United States of America. She formed an opinion. The circumstances that involved their treatment of me were so bizarre and unabashedly unacceptable and in violation of what a reasonable and prudent man would do. That's the extent to which we as Christians in God's Church we're treating one another. It was so alarming that she was compelled to act on it. She gave the pastor a Sunday date and demanded that he stand in his pulpit and publicly apologize for the manner in which I was treated and further place me back into all positions I held prior to these events. She further ordered me to immediately notify her if this demand was not honored. 33 years ago, and it has not yet been honored. In dismay, I chose not to respond to her because I felt that the Church of God was at a serious impasse.

To honor the Spirit of Christ in forgiveness, the foremost reason for the cross and simply saying, I'm sorry was nowhere in sight. The command of God himself to obey the laws of the land in Romans and the sermon on the Mount in Matthews was not even worthy of consideration. Six of the most powerful words ever spoken in the threads of forgiveness are" I admit I made a mistake".

Hurting like hell, I was standing in church and out of church. I was fighting to do the right thing. clear my name and restore my integrity. I would never give up. I would never accept defeat. I was in too deep.

Against the forces and powers of evil, how can I sit and say nothing? And when I stand, I am ridiculed and humiliated. From a mere question of interest, to sit down and shut up. The serious battles that I have been mandated to stand and fight for, or have chosen to stand and fight for, have been huge. It seems that at every turn I have failed and suffered extensively. How much more? How long God? What was really required of me? When will this pattern end? While the origins of all of my battles are unselfish, the conclusions I am blamed for. My strong held expectations that justice, righteousness, fairness, honesty and veracity are character traits that should be exemplified in God's Church, not man's, ended up with me being a problem. What should God's Church look like in 2021? Supporting, loving, nurturing and being considerate and concerned about the heartfelt spirit of God's children concluded that I was a troublemaker. And thus, I have accepted the responsibility that if in fact, in my pursuit to do right, I'm wrong, then so let it be. The Bible and the spirit of Christ speaks for itself. I am just an agent or willing vessel of that doctrine. Let justice roll down like waters and righteousness like a mighty stream. When the world orders the church to do the right thing, God is not glorified.

On two occasions I was considered for the position of pastor and was rejected both times. I suppose that my great work did not speak for me. My untiring and consistent contributions were of no value. It was not why I was doing these great works but that I had done these great works. Seemingly, what mattered was the stigma that doing good in the world and standing on God's word in the church awarded me in the end.

LET THE WORKS THAT I'VE DONE STILL SPEAK FOR ME.

In church and outside of church, my life was devastated. It was rapidly depleting, deteriorating and the quality of life that God ordained for all of us was diminishing. And I couldn't stop it. Holding on or Letting go was now the biggest decision I would ever make. Which would render the best result? I was stunned and suspended in mid animation. Jesus hung on the cross, for his cause and purpose. He held on until he died. But I had a harsh wakeup call and reality. I wasn't Jesus. I Let Go. I stepped down and trusted that in his own divine time, my change would come.

The battle was overwhelming, embarrassing, and weakening. My mission and dream were destroyed. My church relationship for 20 years was shattered and my family was in despair. One Sunday, on the way home after service in my station wagon taxi cab, finally in a state and tone of utter exhaustion, one child asked," do we have to go back there again?"

When we arrived home, my wife came upstairs where I was sitting. Laid her head on my lap and while sobbing in deep despair, she said" I can't do it anymore". Maybe, feeling that she was disappointing my determination to stand my ground at whatever cost, I don't know. We never discussed it again. I was and have always been outspoken, courageous and a fighter. But this time, I realized that as the leader of my family of nine I could no longer subject them to this excruciating pursuit of honor, integrity and dignity at my expense.

I LET GO

...Against my desire and my warring spirit.

Against my trust that God was going to work it out.

Against my determination to stand for what is good right and pleasing in God's sight

I realized that Holding on had now taken an adverse effect.

Holding on was now a trick of the enemy to kill, steal and destroy.

I RELEASED IT ALL

I LET GO AND I LET GOD

HOLD ON AND DIE OR LET GO LIVE

Chapter 7

ORDER MY STEPS
Psalms 119:133

T he greatest decision one can make in life is accepting Christ to be
Lord and savior in their hearts and in so doing, trusting that his
written word (Bible) will become a guiding light and inspiration in
their lives. In life our decisions are often formulated or guided by our
pains, disappointments, experiences and the influences others have in
our choices. Man, what others think and do as they are established in our
portfolios from birth, crack babies, parental guidance and ongoing
learned behavior at vulnerable stages has a serious effect on our rational
and mental processing as we develop. They all affect our ability to think
clearly, fairly, honorably and intelligently. Because of God's vast
resources and knowledge of who we are, why we are, what we are, he
sees our fate and daily realities long before we experience them. Only he
really has our genuine best interest at heart all the time and is

uninterrupted by issues that are not directly ours but only adhere to the path set for our destiny.

Sidebar. There is a favorite cliche of mine that says, "all that I am or ever hope to be, I owe to those who helped me along life's way". Caution! Their spirit and agendas tend to influence their contributions to us.

God wants that we would not only live and thrive for the basic tenancies, tendencies and ability to make ends meet and just to get by, but his desire for us in life is that we should have that more abundantly. More than conquerors. Blessed, pressed down, shaken together and running over. He wants to show off his mighty works in and through us.

While he gives us the ability in Ecclesiastes 7:8, to consider the end, for the end of a thing is better than the beginning. Think things through. Think before you speak. Shut up and listen. Write the vision and make them plain, plan to execute and execute the plan. However, we live through life blindly, not knowing what lies ahead. There are often distractions, impromptu and unplanned interruptions and oppositional spirits on attack to take you off course. Jeremiah 29:11 discloses that I know the plans that I have for you. Plans of peace and not of evil, to give you an expected end. A good end. He knows better how to direct our paths because he knows our end. He's best equipped to give us instructions on how to proceed. When to make a right instead of a left. When to yield, slow down and proceed with caution. Make a U-turn or simply stay on the assigned route. He orders our steps that we might not be swayed by every wind of doctrine.

Who goes on a camping trip or Into the Wilderness of life without a flashlight? Who builds a car without headlights and high beams When it gets too dark and you're on the road alone and can't see around the bend? His word is a lamp. It is a light that illuminates, brightens, directs and points you on your path so that you can see more clearly and discern what's not always visible. It penetrates the dark. His word empowers you to break through and tear down strongholds and expose hidden traps and motives. Let his word be a flashlight that makes your pathway accessible as you tread through the dark and unknown challenges that confront you. Psalms 119:105 says that his word is a lamp unto my feet and a light unto my path.

As you journey toward that good and your destined end, going forward, allow his word to order your steps.

Chapter 8

My Second Church
2000-2004

I n 2000 my 20 year membership with my first church had come to a
painful and disrespectful end as much as I tried to avoid it. My father
died of colon cancer. My mother's desire for her son's was that we
began to practice preventive care. Colonoscopies and the like. We had
decided to take a breather from the church experience. Recoup and
recover I suppose. For twenty years it had become an essential aspect of
living. Sunday morning. Sunday evening. Sunday nights sometimes. Bible
study, cutting the grass, cleaning the bathroom, tidying up the pulpit,
transporting, preaching, singing, teaching, praying, counseling and any
other assignment and request.

I guess I was possibly overwhelmed and didn't even know it. I just knew that I loved Jesus, he had delivered me and he said, go to church. God said it. I believed it. That settles it kind of thing. You know? Like the commercial years ago with the egg in the frying pan sizzling and the narrator says," this is your brain on drugs". Any questions? That's how I was with God. It's just Jesus. Case dismissed.

I welcomed the break as I believe that my family did also. Although it felt strange, it was refreshing to just get up on Sunday and go or not go. No pressure. What a relief. We visited different churches for a while but soon became concerned that our children were not actively engaged in church life and activities in particular. I asked one of my teens at my first church once why he came to Bible study so consistently. He says, because it keeps me focused. As his Youth Leader, I was so impressed with that answer and it was our concern for our children's regular involvement. Out of sight, out of mind if you can feel me. After a couple of months, we felt that they needed to be in a little more stabilized environment as it was a serious part of their life's foundation. Most of our discussion centered around my second Church. They had attended there several times and liked the environment. We all had begun to enjoy both Pastor's style of preaching and clarity in their teaching. The spirit among the members was also inviting. Several Sundays passed and one Sunday at invitation time without any further discussion or pressure, I stood and they all stood simultaneously. That was an awesome example of unity and being on one accord. We needed their lifestyles to be inclusive of God and worship with others of like faith.

I made it perfectly clear to the pastor of this church that I had absolutely no interest in performing any leadership duties or participating in any ministerial projects. I was tired. I had been through a 20-year experience and I simply wanted to sit down, hear God's word, and allow my children to continue to develop as Christians. I did not want, and neither was I going to get involved and I was clearly adamant. As we continued in fellowship, he made a request to use my children's experience to help him formulate a choir. I was in agreement and because Of their prior singing experience they were honored to assist. I really enjoyed the preached word on Sundays and didn't mind at all driving 40 minutes to service. My journey had been long, painful and extensive. I was inspired by the growth of this church and began to befriend and bond with its members. I have always been approachable, simple and down-to-earth, and filled with dry humor. Very dry humor. That means that I tried to be funny but it was clearly not an attribute that I possessed. The members liked me and began to draw to me and my family My sister had been there for a while and was very well known among them. One Sunday after service, the pastor asked to speak privately with me and I think my third wife at the time. His request was that I organize a Youth Education Ministry. I was much older than him and he felt that because of my history as a Director of the Youth Ministry, it would be a great asset in their growth. Very hesitant and reluctantly I offered my assistance. My wife and I were a powerful team and a force to reckon with when we were on the same accord.

We began to put a program together that would meet his request. He needed a Bible study, worship-oriented program during each service, during the preaching hour. This included 8 am and 11 am on Sundays, Wednesday nights at 7:30 p.m. and all other times there was preaching involved. We packaged and assembled study material for three age groups, three times per week, for 18 teachers, with their choice of age groups and their choice of days and times to teach. Truth be told, that was an awesome program. Now that I think about it. We also provided each teacher with Advanced material for 90 days. A full teaching schedule for a 90-day cycle. The organization and implementation was something to behold by someone who sincerely did not want to be bothered. Preach to me, use my service to God's glory and I'm out of here. The church was in awe at how well established this project was. I was amazed, and while it was in full operation during every service, my wife and I were in regular church service enjoying the worship and praise.

The pastor was in such awe that one Sunday while I was helping to set up for an event, he approached me. He asked, how do you so effectively execute a project while sitting in service every week? I said to him. You asked me to set it up and manage it, not do it. Managing, organizing and executing is what I was accustomed to doing and now the talk of the Church was no longer centered around its two pastors. It was how awesome Pastor Mac was. They began to compare us to David and Saul and Saul's jealousy of how blessed David was. Saul killed 1000 but David killed 10,000. Saul was so jealous of David and enraged, that he tried to literally set him up and kill him on many occasions. It was starting to grow out of control. Even now, as a reader of my memoir you can discern the trend. Here comes Satan. I did what you asked me, and I did it well, and now you are hating on me. Unfortunately, jealousy and envy can grasp us so quickly and unconsciously and they are the most dangerous weapons in Satan's arsenal, especially in God's Church and then it leads to deadly competition.

Jealousy and envy were now rearing its ugly head again and I didn't even want to do it. If I don't do my best, I have to answer to God and if I do my best, I get beat down by man. Lord help us.

Just that quick, my popularity had become my problem and because of my desire to please God and my willingness to sacrifice for others even when it's not in my best interest. The church and their ministries were thriving. Families were increasing because teachers were excited, children were learning, and parents were free to worship and praise in peace. A perfect combination and it was all because of, "THE MAC" families and children were growing and worshipping together, WOW, Heaven is rejoicing. In my discernment and the consensus among some of the pastor's leadership, he wanted to confine and put me in lockdown so that I wouldn't be in service to offset my gifts of managing God's Property and program. I got it because God gave it to me. I am fearfully and wonderfully made, and I know that quite well. Psalm 139:14. Remember, I believe what he said. I love Jesus and I can't help but to please him and do all that I do to his Glory. 1st Corinthians 10: 22 -33. For if I by grace be a partaker. Why am I evil spoken of? Whether therefore, ye eat, or drink, or whatever you do, do all to the glory of God. For by him, in him, and through him, I have my being. I am sorry. He's that kind of friend. Romans 11:36.

In my spirit, I was now being visited by my first church experience and should have immediately jumped ship, but now I'm responsible, accountable and connected to this wonderful body of loving people whose aspirations are escalated. And my children and wife are devotedly busy at work again. So I suppressed what I knew was on the rise again. I maintained my role in managing the task that I had organized and we continued to perfect it. I attended service diligently as I had for more than a year before I accepted this task. I did not engage in any further activity. Later, the pastor felt a need to ordain me in the preaching ministry again. However, I believe he did that to make amends or to establish criteria for monetary gain and accolades. In any case, they preached, I heard great preaching and my family continued to serve as they had been accustomed for years. As the Temptations would say, "and the band played on", the church rolled on.

In the Christmas season of 2003, my wife and I were asked to present a Christmas program. We worked on that project so perfectly together that I was amazed at our teamwork. Considering our ongoing challenges as husband and wife. where jealousy was also an evident presence. It was no doubt a monumental success. There was a real infant child in the manger as Jesus. All of the hay was real and a mess to clean up. The color orchestration and participation from each Ministry was superb. There was an air of joy and delight all over the church that night. The church was packed with standing room only. I was directing and my wife was in the background making sure every scene was enacted with precision. A heavenly spotlight illuminated around the baby as wise men brought gifts. At the end every performer gathered around the manger and sang with the excitement like you've never seen; "

Go Tell It on the Mountain,

Over the hills and everywhere.

Go Tell It on the Mountain,

That Jesus Christ is born.

All of the Lights except the one around Jesus was dimmed to Darkness and they were slowly raised up with an arousing applause and standing ovation.

While I, the director said: For unto us this day in the city of David, a child is born and his name shall be called Jesus.

The in-house reviews for weeks to follow were filled with hope, accolades and a sense of great accomplishment throughout the church and those who witnessed the presentation. The recommendations were made to the leaders that we take the show on the road. Hollywood here we come. I must admit that it was an astonishing display of talent, and no doubt, I was in trouble again.

The show began to dominate conversations and Pastor Mack was the highlight of praise. Jealousy and Envy toward me was now taken to another level. As hard as it was, I chose not to engage in or respond to all of the attention and adverse spirits that were flaring up all around me. I simply did what I was asked. My popularity grew immensely and was now causing separation and friction added to all of the other issues this church was experiencing which I was taking a blind eye to.I was there for my children and a Word of Inspiration and everything else was not my concern.

When I arrived at this church in 2000 and chose to make our membership there, several other close family and Associates joined me. We had now reached a point when we had met to discuss the possibility of starting our own church and the contributions that we could make to the Kingdom by way of our experiences. We all had experienced so many things that just didn't line up with what I believe God meant or wanted for or in his house of worship. We had met and decided to pray and seek God's guidance for 30 days and there were about thirty of us.

And here we were once again at the negative highlight of my tenure there. Totally engulfed in opposition, accusations, control, favoritism, disrespect, jealousy and envy and being used. We were now led to consider God's will for our lives going forward. In the heat of being used, regulated, suppressed and limited in all of my gifts, convictions and desires for Jesus, the man I love, I felt my departure and demise taking form. I did all I could for others in spite of my original opposition and I do it to the best of my ability and now all of my good is being evil spoken of. I've actually never been blamed for doing good, I've been blamed because of how it made others look and feel.

All of my step-children's fathers hated my guts, not because of my good work but because of how my good works made them look. Image scarred again. Accusation again. Jealousy and envy again. Lying on me and discrediting my name again. I could not engage. I simply wrote a letter to the Pastor's, and said: "I believe that I have fulfilled my duty here and am led at this time to establish a church as pastor. Those who accompanied me when I arrived will be assisting me in this endeavor. They believed in me and my vision for God's Church. My tenure here must come to an end. Thank you for accepting my family and I and allowing us to be a part of this great ministry. All the best". I never entered his church again and he never responded to my professional presentation of one of like faith and responsibility. To whom much is given, much is required. However, he claimed that I had undermined his Ministry and stole his members. Some of which had left him long before I had even contemplated the move. He never spoke positively of me

again or thank me for the work that I had contributed at his bequest.

As we moved forward to erect this mission for God, we committed to be mindful, sensitive and considerate of God's Will and love for his people. We vowed that we would never allow all the serious issues that we had all experienced as Christians to play or penetrate Christ Church under our leadership.

The slanderous characterizations and attacks on my integrity and image, as humiliating, unfair, ungrateful, accusation and condemning as they were: I chose not to hold onto in my heart as long as I had in the past.

Harboring no ill-will, anger or animosity, I SIMPLY LET GO..........

HOLD ON AND DIE OR LET GO AND LIVE

Chapter 8

Sermonic Lesson

LIFE'S VICIOUS CYCLE
2 Corinthians 4:8-12

Y ou've heard the old cliche "you don't have to tell me but one time". This is not always the case. More often we hear, "if I told you once, I've told you a thousand times" or," how many times do I have to repeat myself". How about the question, why do I have to keep telling you the same thing over and over again? It almost seems generational, not only among children which we understand and expect rebellion, but also among adults who keep repeating the same mistakes, Time after time and time again. It's like a deadly uncontrollable cycle. Years ago, there was a saying attached to an automobile manufacturer." fix or repair daily." You figure that out. The implication is that if you don't fix what is broken, it will break or malfunction again. And even more so, some mistakes will cost you more if you continue to repeat them. If you are constantly repairing the same damage, fixing what you broke yesterday, today, then lessons are costing you double or triple what is necessary. Also, life and opportunities are slowly ticking away. Life is filled with mistakes. It's called growth and human development, but if we don't learn from those mistakes, we are doomed to repeat them.

Life, Satan, people or even family often set traps for a multitude of reasons and if we're not on our game, we will fall into them. I would like to share an analogy if you would pardon me of humans and rats, or better still mice. A mouse or rat will never get caught the second time in a trap if he ever gets out. Even if what he went for the first time is put back on it. It's a built-in mechanism of self-preservation at all costs. Maybe it's the route to the trap, the smell, the sound or the close encounters associated with the experience. Google it. Do your homework and be guided accordingly. But you will never catch him in that same trap. If we can possibly learn to get it right the first time, we can move on. Isn't that good news?

We can't maintain consistent growth in life if there's always setbacks. If you don't pass the test today, you will have to take it again, possibly on tomorrow. There is a chronological method to the madness. We can't go to college at five years old and the first grade at 19 years old. The steps in life are designed to go up and not down. Forward and not backwards. Airplanes, which get us where we want and need to go faster than most methods of transportation are usually not built with a reverse gear. In order to go backwards, they have to be pushed.

Trials come to make us stronger, better, and wiser. In many cases, the judge will give you a nice slap on the wrist for a first offense while he warns that if you come back for the same reason, the consequences will be greater. If you don't get it the first time, you will suffer more the second time. and so on and so on as life slowly dwindles away. History and statistics have shown that when one gets out of jail and returns back to the same environment their reality is inevitable and our records begin to hinder us from a breakthrough and path to victory.

Obstacles repeated becomes our detriment. Most of our pitfalls in life occur when there is no change in how we process simple issues and mistakes that should normally empower us. We learn by mistakes. In this text the Apostle Paul is inviting us not to be overtaken by his sufferings and pain but to gain from them. We can enhance our lives by learning from others. He said we suffer because we preach, but you can benefit from our preaching and suffering. We can learn from our forefathers who took 40 years to make an 11-day journey and died in the wilderness because they came out of bondage and never changed their behavior. They became trapped in and died in their wilderness because they just kept doing things the same way over and over again. Change is not only inevitable it is necessary.

Dr. King in one of his speeches stated that you cannot use Ox cart methods in a jet age. When we get trapped in these vicious cycles, it is the blood of Jesus that keeps us, sustains us, empowers and directs us to break through life's vicious cycles. We have been redeemed from the curse but it is only by the blood of Jesus that we can be restored whole again.

Christ died only once and for all. He did not have to keep dying over and over again. All it takes for us to break from these constant pitfalls in life is that we get it, for the sooner we get that, the better off we will all be.

Chapter 9

My Third Church Shammah ministries 2004-2018

I n the process of preparing this 50-year memoir, I became shockingly aware that at the age of 51 I was about to embark on this awesome task of building a business for God. Erecting a church, an entity that had the potential of transforming lives. Altering and changing behavior. Restoring and redeeming the very soul of man. I was the leader of the pack. The agent, Angel and Authority. I would be the shepherd. The guiding light and the link between Heaven and Earth. Called, set apart and anointed to represent God himself while leading all to him. Changing lives by example.

I had been in church since 1980, serving, helping and learning. But this time the ultimate course of its fate rested on me. I would be the one looked upon to reflect the character, conduct and conversation of Christ. The Savior of the world. The Christ that I had learned about his cross in 1980 while I was on my cross. Jesus, the Christ who had helped, loved, saved and delivered me from my crisis. And I felt destined for the challenge and awesome responsibility. For 24 years I had seen and personally experienced much pain and disappointment when his Spirit, his word and his presence is not honored, accepted and practiced. But I was in no way leery of the road ahead.

I loved him. He was real and I was ready. Immediately upon leaving my second Church, 30 of us sat down after 30 days of prayer and began the development of God's Church. Its name was, Shammah Ministries 21st Century Church. Shammah was one of King David's Mighty Warriors. He stood up against the Philistines and God brought Victory through him. I also am a warrior which I'm sure you can surmise by now. The 21st century represents this present age. Preaching and teaching the power of the oldest word in history, simply and soundly to the newest generation, without changing even a comma.

I had the profound privilege of erecting his house (the church) and executing his will in it. And I had gone through enough hell to know what heaven looked like. After 24 years I didn't have all the wisdom and knowledge on what to do, but I had learned what not to do. I was told once that life is a gift from God, and what you do with it is a gift to God. I had learned of him. Believed in him and lived by him. I have found a simple and successful principal in this task and that is to love the way Christ loved. live the way Christ lived and lead the way Christ did. I considered this a simple formula to guide me.

1. Unconditionally. 2. He looked beyond my faults.3. He died even while I was sinning.

I envisioned what God's church should look like in real time so that I would always have an image in my mind. A path to pursue. A portrait to periodically reflect upon.

I was sitting by the pool one day at a resort very close to the beach. and the scene was breathtaking. The ocean was aqua. The pool was pristine blue. The waves were soothing and relaxing. A slight wind was blowing against me. There was drinking at the bars. People were playing ball, wearing speedos, bikinis, and two-piece swimwear. Conversations were held in different languages. Big people, little people, short people, tall people, old people, young people, white people, black people. swimming, running, dancing, laughing, crying, kayaking, skydiving, fishing, music playing, singing, host serving individual needs. Such a serene scene. Peaceful, no yelling, screaming, arguing, or cursing. All in one place, at one time, together, on one accord, living their best life. Many members, one body, all operating as one harmonious and melodious whole family. I am sure you've all been there. I closed my eyes. I embraced the atmosphere, listened to all of the sounds, ocean, music, conversations and the wind and I thought, I imagined, that this is what God's Church should look like. If I could only build a church that looked like what it sounded like in my ear. Truly God would be glorified. Wishful thinking, I know. Yes, maybe even a little naive, but a model to behold. This was the Kodak moment that compelled my every movement and journey as a pastor. A bouquet of flowers beautifully arranged in a vase with every fragrance (personality) and type contributing to and illuminating its completeness. That serene scene. Beauty was in unity, not individuality. But compacted and empowered by that which every joint (person) supplieth (Ephesians 4:16).

I knew that my personal relationship with Jesus would be the essential element in executing this paramount vision and my ability to rally a team of committed souls in the leadership would be step number one. Their devotion to serve God and His members to the end was also predicated on their convictions and love for him. We simply had to be on the same page. I had to constantly convey that mandate. My DNA and spirit as an Under Shepherd is what had to fuel and visibly display and define what role I was to play and how. My DNA and spirit were simple even though my character was sometimes unorthodox, complex and technical. It was all aligned in his word, his will and his way. I believed that in all of my actions and intent that I was to literally reflect Jesus as I knew him and as he had shown himself to me. My sacrifices for all who were placed under my spiritual authority became indelibly interwoven with his sacrifices. His unconditional love for me defined every thread of my heart and leadership to others, and I was crucified and rejected as He was and that's what I was determined to exemplify in my walk and that's what got me crucified.

The beginning process after 30 of us met was to ensure that as the first family of the church, they shared my love for God's people, their willingness to stand for and with them in their growth and development stages as Christians, and to partner with me on the strategies and exampleship that I was led, not as they saw or perceived it, but as I was led to embrace and execute it. After all, as pastor, I was the link that connected God to His church. This was our first and biggest challenge and catastrophe. I required no pressure and held them as my family to no great responsibility. I required them to love me and support me in this cause as I had loved and supported our family in their cause. The main calling and qualification to care for God's Church is based on how you cared for your own family.

I waited until every responsibility to my family had been fulfilled before I accepted this great privilege of now raising up a family for God. Even their attendance was not mandated by me. They were adults and they had the same freewill as did all. Whosoever will, let him come. However, in leadership, to whom much is given, much is required. As leaders there must be a higher standard of life style. When things began to turn in their expected behavior, if and when they came, I found myself reiterating, if you are not going to help me, don't hurt me, just stay away because the behavior role and image of the first family is exemplary. It can be very destructive as I have shared in previous chapters.

Our first place of worship for four years was in a public school where cleanliness and order were not our friends. We were blessed after that tenure for four years to serve at a sorority hall where I was employed for 13 years and my duty was to set up and break down all events. The cost to worship there was a welcomed expense. As a source of revenue to support Shammah. I established what was becoming a very successful Monday Night Bingo project. In the Christian realm, gambling was now visited as one of those unorthodox character traits that I possessed. I remember Malcolm and his "by any means necessary stand" but it did not quite blend with Christian orthodox. It was good money, but I yielded because of controversy. In any case, because I wasn't obliged to partner with some of the leaders there at the sorority hall, It ultimately resulted in a distasteful relationship that not only concluded my employment, but a sudden untimely departure of our church.

Grateful to God, no matter the circumstances, we found ourselves in an undesired location for worship in Capitol Heights, Maryland for three months. Expressing a sincere discomfort to continue worship in what was referred to as a little hole-in-the-wall, we found a wonderful space in a shopping center in District Heights, Maryland. The cost was a bit steep but all agreed to support me in securing this space and the potential it afforded us in ministry. Stepping out on faith, trust and limited resources, my wife and I signed a five-year lease. This move was contingent upon every man of the church committing to participate in a project that would secure our ability to move. However, after a short stay there, every man reneged on their support and contributions and left me in a very dangerous struggle to maintain that monthly expense. The abandonment of their commitment and support now after only four months there introduced a serious demise in the confidence and trust that I forestated was key in fulfilling this vision. As an angel whose eyes must always be open, I'm clearly not liking what I'm discerning. Under pressure or a temporary fulfillment of excitement, people will leave you at the drop of a hat. But I am now bound by a lease, not for self-aggrandizement, but out of my love for Jesus, I put my life on the line again. I didn't want to be paid. I never did think that I deserved to be paid for the work I did for God. I didn't get it until the eighth year in ministry. I gave and only received if there was something left. We continued in worship there and grew to 150 members.

The vision was becoming visible. Bible study and retreats, a desire to learn and acquire a closer walk with God was blossoming in the body. Dance ministry and the praise team were rising up and enlightening the course to fulfilling this vision. Fellowship with one another was sought and enjoyed. The church was growing. The word was spreading, Shammah was the place to be. The spirit among God's people was elevating. We were developing resources to sustain the ministry. Money was no longer coming out of my pocket. Neighboring businesses were watching and inquiring. Even the landlord was respecting and paying tribute to the concept of church and his relationship with a "genuine" pastor. Our image and the disappointment he had encountered before us was changing. We were restoring the image of the shopping center and engaging in community projects. Our church's previous tenant was a club that ended in murder, prostitution, and an eyesore to the county. We converted filth into favor with God.

Our church space was flooded with weddings, receptions, conferences, prayer breakfasts, anniversaries. We participated in a community baptism in North Beach, Maryland where we baptized 55 Christians outdoors. We participated with a community project on Thanksgiving giving away over 800 Thanksgiving dinners.

Because of the great gifts and talents that comprised our membership, social events and plays were created and directed with highly recognized accolades. We were a church on the rise and the vision was being realized.

In this short-lived move of God, I had married over 36 couples with a history of only one couple failing. Counseling had developed into my main gift, and had become widely recognized as a vital resource in relationship development.

I was crossing my T's.

I was dotting my I's.

I was treading carefully.

I was minding my own business.

I was taking responsibility for my own actions.

I was living right.

I was honoring God.

I was helping man.

I was hosting baby showers, buying school clothes and books, paying electric bills and rent, supporting weddings and receptions, buying food, cars, gas, and paying telephone bills. For the most part, I was doing all of this outreach with the many blessings God was sending my way. Rarely with church funds or personal income.

At all cost, I was avoiding controversy, criticism, chaos, condemnation and gossip. I was almost there. I was loving as Christ instructed. I was living as Christ instructed. I was working as Christ instructed. I was letting this mind be in me that was also in Christ Jesus. I was letting my light so shine that men may see my good works and glorify God. I was steadfast and unmovable, always abounding in the work of the Lord, knowing that my labor was not in vain. I was diligently seeking him. I was seeking him first in all things. I was simply sold out and serious about this call to mission and vision. I had gone through and lost too much to repeat business as usual.

My sacrifices were starting to pay off. I can taste it. I can feel it. I could see glimpses of the vision. It was not in vain. In my heart, I was the epitome of Christ. I know this because I went to bed at night and woke up in the morning, purposed, poised, promulgated, planning and perfecting his will in my life. Because it was real and I accepted it with Grace. I was human but I was heaven bound.

Once again, my popularity was increasing and the trend was changing, but there was an undercurrent developing. Something was beginning to unveil and cause a major deterioration in the professional ethics we practiced and the quality and substance of life we exemplified. Family issues were now starting to transcend into the church and our image was under severe attack. At the helm and forefront of the issues that had begun to undermine the core values of unconditional love, compassion and unity were family and leadership.

Churches are anointed and appointed to minister to, confront and address humanitarian needs of every sort, but we were now overwhelmed, and leaders and family were managing on their own accord and not in the spirit of the pastor. Everybody started doing their own thing. And now discipline and correction by the pastor was being rebelled against. Everybody was okay as long as they were allowed to do whatever they wanted to and now the spirit of unity and being on one accord is threatened. I was starting to receive signals reflecting just how much respect my family and leadership staff had for my authority. Publicly, it was all about the pastor. Privately, it was all about their agenda.

This mindset started sweeping through the woodwork of every

ministry. "Do what I want or I'm leaving" was the underlying threat from family and leaders, because they know or think that I cannot survive without them. Lifestyles outside of church were not in alignment with expectations and examples in the church that God required. Their behavior exemplified godliness in the church and worldliness outside of the church. They were beginning to smile in my face while digging a sharp knife into my back. They were straddling the fence in other words. They had one step in heaven and one step in hell. Sadly, most of them thought that I could not see through their facades.

They never could tell what I was thinking. They were working in total opposition against me, sending mixed signals to those they had favor with. Showing fellowship and favoritism with whom they slept, drank and partied with and judgment, criticism and ridicule with whom they worshiped with and called to serve in the spirit of Christ. Their positions and work in the church was for self-aggrandizement and in disrespect for the pastor and office of the pulpit.

I realized that it was happening again. The Devil was starting his pattern of sifting me like wheat. I was under attack again and he was simply using them as pawns in his game to destroy me and subsequently the vision that God had given me to turn all of my good into evil and turn all of my blessings into curses. Like a dimmer switch that you can turn up and turn down at will, using all the sources available for his influence. Every time I tried to soar, he would construct a means to pull me down and now he had started again using everyone around me at his disposal.

How did I live every day with a constant force of opposition always finding a way to penetrate and pierce my heart and corrupt my intent? Angels of Darkness all around me, pulling me down, oil on my wings weighing me down so that I can't soar and rise to that destination that God ordained high in Heavenly places? And, here we go again. I would imagine that one sure way of determining if Satan is using you is if you keep your mind stayed on Jesus. Otherwise you are simply easy prey. My sister, my praise worshipper and warrior, leader and prophet, whom I licensed, left me after I said no to her the first and only time in 30 years of support. She walked out on me when she couldn't have her way with me. She faked God more than she favored God and it was becoming evident throughout the ministry. Her devoted friend and confidant who was the director of my praise team manipulated her departure after that in an elegant and tasteful Godly form. Of course, the Lord directed the move. It is amazing and amusing how we use God to substantiate our fleshly agendas. They often disrespected or just disregarded my authority. On an occasion I was threatened by these leaders who were agents of the unconditional love and saving grace of Christ when I embraced a relative of transgender status into membership. I licensed them. I loved them. I helped them and made great sacrifices for them. They used me and then dropped me like hot coal. In the name of Jesus always. Their agendas and behavior began to filter down into the ministry and sow discord in my ability to lead God's people unconditionally, fairly and peacefully against their influence and perceived relationships with God. Their perspective had become a stumbling block and in no way did it project a welcoming embrace to whosoever will, let him come.

In our neighboring circle and community, the image and reputation of Shammah was under attack and the authenticity of its leadership tested and under scrutiny. My nephew who was a practicing homosexual approached me one day and asked me if I would license him to preach the gospel. I informed him that in addition to the character, conversation, conduct and knowledge, his lifestyle must also reflect God's word, and his word does not condone homosexuality. His word, not mine. Just like I could not knowingly license a liar, a murderer or a thief, I could not authenticate him in that office. I could not work against God and consider myself His agent. Interestingly, he said that all of his friends were being licensed by their pastors. The enemy was using every resource and act that he could to shift, sift, and twist me in every issue to stain my love for Christ and determination to do his will by starting internal battles, and that it did. I was under attack again by family and leadership. Those who started out with me and vowed to honor and support me in the administration of God's word, will and way had changed their course. Leadership must reflect an example of the lifestyle that God desires for his people. The life he chose to practice or live did not reflect that example. I loved him and I helped raise him. But I could not authenticate him in that office just as I could not accept or engage in the behavior of my family and leadership staff.

It hurt me in the end. My duty and commitment to the vision was to lead according to his word, his will, and his way, not mine, and I tried to stay focused and not coerced into doing what was typical and convenient in this Christian industry, not what the masses were doing and in standing on His doctrine. I've found myself in a desolate place. The word is not designed to line up with our lives or desires. Our lives are requested to line up with his word. I don't like his way all the time, but I am called to represent it. In season and out of season. When it feels good and when it hurts like hell. Let your lights so shine that men may see your good works and glorify God. That light is God's glory, not your story.

Many challenges had begun to confront me as this undercurrent continued to surge out of control. One of my Evangelists, and her two children, were being stalked and were in serious danger. I rushed to her rescue, secured temporary living and kept close watch over her image as an Evangelist and stored her belongings in my office. She was licensed by me and had to have been with me for eight years. I considered her spirit to be a great reflection of true evangelism and I respected it accordingly. She was young, pretty, with two children. She was very close to me as I had become the father she never had. She and I addressed each other with what I was told later was a term of endearment. I called her "slim". We befriended years before she joined under my pastoral leadership.

She was deeply possessed with demons. Cora, was the main demon which was identified by another minister on my staff at a women's program in my home. We were transforming souls. Our work is serious, not a game. For we wrestle not against flesh and blood, but spiritual wickedness in high places. In service, she would crawl on the floor between chairs slobbering with saliva and blood seeping out of her mouth onto the floor. A frightening scene. Those demons were cast out one night at our second church location. What a great testimony for a young pastor knowing that a spirit of power and deliverance existed in his ministry. I connected with her and supported her back to life. A moment of celebration and rejoicing at the awesome transforming work of the Holy Spirit was transformed into an evil spirit of jealousy that ended up with me being accused of fathering her children. How low can you go?

Jealousy, envy and control over me seems to have always been the disease that has caused my lifetime of dis-ease and used against me as weapons of mass destruction. The stage of my mother's dementia was increasing. My angel (God daughter), whom I met when she was five years old at my second church, was in college. My mother needed help and she agreed to go to school during the day and spend the nights to care for her. She was very precious to me and I could trust her to care for my mother, who was also a deacon at my church. My sister, the Prophet, discredited her and my wife accused me of an unhealthy relationship with a student almost 40 years my youth. Every good and decent blessing and gift from God turned into evil by my leadership staff.

At times, there just seemed to be no escape in sight. Anyone who was close to me or anyone I needed to manage my many responsibilities were under constant attacks and treated accordingly. It felt like a force or a conspiracy to ensure my failure at every turn. I never gave up hope. I never gave up on anyone. I loved and embraced all. It was just who I became after I met the MAN. There is an old gospel hymn that says, "I know I've been changed, the angels in heaven done signed my name". I helped all that were under my spiritual authority and gave indication. Barring none. I think I've learned my lesson. I tried to trust all in as much as my spirit would allow me. I stayed focused. I had faith in all. While I was engaged in the struggle, I guess I was in machine mode. Writing about it, I wonder how I endured it. I dreamed big and worked hard and long. I have been on a mission since the age of 16 and I was determined to make it happen, in spite of the odds and the opposition.

I didn't know that it was draining and strangling me. In the process of time, pastoring, preaching, teaching, counseling and working were evolving. My needs were innumerable and my potential was escalating.

In our small church family, nine babies were born in 15 months. My image as a pastor was attached to that statistic and so was the possibility of fathering some of them. There was never any escaping the judgments, condemnation and assertions I experienced in God's Holy Institution where humans dwelled. Men would have died to be what I was perceived and accused of being. I'm just saying.

Jealousy and envy are tools of Satan. They were like a slow wind that swept through my home and church. Inconspicuously injected through every act, issue, decision and programmed into the veins of membership and I watched it corrupt the respect, image and authority of my Ministry. Undermining, sowing discord and planting seeds of destruction. Outright warfare. And at the origin and core of its operation was my family who owned me in their deliverance. The deeply rooted fear of losing what they never had, but because of pride would never admit. I understand and I forgive them for not being able to detect and control it.

But as Satan begins to travel through the universe seeking whom he may devour with jealousy and envy as his weapons, capitalizing on weakness and fear, his ultimate plot against me is about to take its course. For they will protect their image at all costs even at the risk of destroying others.

Years ago, my image and credibility were attacked. Out of vengeance and envy a member of the church that I was pastoring was called from Mexico and informed that I was not performing my manly duties. I had walking pneumonia for 30 days. Thick, green mucus like clay compacted my body. I had a fever. I could not drink or get into the water. I choked as I coughed uncontrollably trying to pull up mucus. No part of my body was functioning, and I was told that I should have been dead. After 15 days of non-effective medical treatment, I arrived home on a Saturday. I preached on Sunday morning and was admitted to Seventh-day Adventist Hospital on Monday morning. The hospital panicked and kept me and performed every conceivable examination to determine why I was not dead. There was a dark green clay substance up to my neck choking me.

A short time later, my image and credibility were attacked, when my wife's older daughter hid the fact that she had given her husband permission to have an outside affair that yielded two children. The sacred office of my call to pastor was used to conceal the truth while I watched my family and church suffer deep pain and humiliation from the perceived trauma inflicted on their loved one and disdain for my insensitive demeanor. I was trying to protect her privacy.

My image and credibility were deeply scarred among those whom I led when my wife's second child demanded the position to manage our professional catering and outreach service to the public. She did not have the qualifications or equipment necessary. When I denied her request, she and her family attacked me and threatened to walk out on my youth ministry and the church. They constantly voiced their disappointment and unfair treatment too many, influencing their respect for my authority and financial commitment to serve in a legal, practical and effective way.

As I had requested from the outset.

My image and credibility were attacked and misrepresented when my wife's son without notice walked out on my Youth and Young Adult Ministry leaving them disappointed. He and his family claimed that I was hindering him from fulfilling a new life with his new wife and their new church. I simply asked for professional protocol and an opportunity to replace him before my youth were left without guidance, instruction and mentorship as they were accustomed and offered by him.

My image and credibility were seriously called into question when my wife's youngest daughter conceived a child out of wedlock. This action and behavior as it had been on many occasions in our church should have remained an intimate and personal matter that took its course in our home. My family chose to incorporate this matter in God's Church using their parents' role as pastor to justify, and excuse their shame, guilt and behavior. Ask God for forgiveness if you feel convicted or if you feel that you have disappointed your God. But you will not use God's house to project your behavior as saintly while you condemn everyone else as a bunch of whores who made booty calls and are now consumed in baby daddy drama. You will not use my office as pastor to degrade and expose the infirmities of others. They played on the sympathy and compassion of God's people and in the process, they seriously stained my image and credibility as an angel of God's house. To this effect, I received a call from someone who, through our genuine experience and declaration of being friends for life, said to me, I apologize for judging you. I had no clue what that meant. That's the profound effect that their actions had on an already dwindling ministry as the first family. It is the responsibility of the pastor and the first family to reflect in our lifestyles an example of God's word and his desire for the lifestyle he wishes us to live. Judgment starts, in the house and at the top (1 Peter 4:17). They knew better, but vengeance, envy, jealousy and rage are weapons Satan uses to destroy the work of Christ and that work was in me.

They were angry with me because I could not engage them in their treatment of another person. I begged them, please stop before there is irreparable damage. However, if you insist on this ungodly Behavior, I cannot continue this journey with you as father or pastor. They could not manipulate me in their hate and lies. They could not sway me from my morals, ethics and integrity. I was accountable to a greater cause. Jesus. Because they had subjected the church to, their manipulating and deceptive tactics, the first lady and the church membership had to choose where their loyalties rested.

My credibility was being destroyed in court and in church. The first lady's loyalties were to her children, not to her husband or the church they led together. I could not support their tactics and agendas at home or in church. The children had already begun because of their disrespect for my position, to walk out of church while I was preaching, influencing members and family against me to this day. All of my resources were depleted. There were only a handful of members now. I could not pay the rent. In a church group text, I was literally begging for support. I had no pride in doing so. The battle was not mine. The damage had been done. Satan had succeeded again. My blood pressure was high. I lost 14 pounds. My wife and I was separated after 25 years of marriage. I was abandoned and alone. I could not carry it all anymore. It had weighed me down now to utter defeat. I needed to release it all and Let It Go. I had stood at the front door of the church for two weeks hoping for a

miracle and trying to develop the courage and strength to not only accept defeat but to announce it.

HOW LONG DO I HOLD ON? WHEN DO I LET GO?

On December 16, 2018 when I stood before the congregation at 10 a.m. I announced that this will be the last sermon that I administer as your Pastor. The devastating sound of silence dominated the air. I was sued by my landlord for $30,000 for terminating the lease early. To protect myself I filed bankruptcy.

This huge personal catastrophe that had occurred in my family had by design transcended into the church family as a weapon against me.It had permeated the entire church without my knowledge or approval by my family, coerced by my wife's daughter in her state of rage and vengeance. They were too weak to stand against her and today we are all suffering the utter chaos of her unsuccessful pursuit to protect her unblemished image. I'm begging again. SOMEBODY HELP HER PLEASE.

How could I fight or avoid what I couldn't see behind the scenes? It was like a snake injecting his Venom on his prey and watching his life weaken and drained of energy for his ultimate consumption. At every turn in her daughter's adult life, her mother had condoned, tolerated and accepted her behavior and not even made an attempt too seriously correct it or trust that I cared enough to confront her on it. When we don't call our children out in an attempt to correct their behavior, especially at their impressionable age, we empower their will and determination to substantiate and authenticate it. And we are now at an impasse. Her daughter's agenda was to enact a vicious attack on me and perpetuate a plan to cover up her exposed imperfection and restore and protect her scarred image. Twenty-five years of marriage and 15 years of Pastoring had merged into an onslaught of hate, revenge, jealousy, envy and rage. She was out of control and her family couldn't stop her, just engage her because of their loyalties. A calculating and collective force of pure evil had now climaxed. Confidence in me as a Pastor among the remaining members had been irreparably damaged by their sensitivity to my daughter's performance. They allowed her to affect them and just took a backseat approach. After all, what did they have to lose? As I had endlessly given to and sacrificed for my family for 25 years, I had done the same for my church for 15 years, as I thought was required by God. She had literally on two occasions sought to kill a man using her own cousins and the advice of an instructor at a gun range while her sisters observed. In my final days, this was the spirit that dominated and fueled evil in my home and in my church. In my life for 50 years, why had I been such a direct target for Satan? At this point, I'm sure that he was rejoicing and all the more, because he used the very people God sent me to salvage.

To this day, they accept no responsibility for my fate as a man, father or a pastor, and they genuinely believe that I brought it all on myself. For 25 years as a husband, father of four children that I didn't birth, and 15 years as a pastor, I gave all that I had, could or imagined, and in the end none of them offered me a hand to help me hold on. They all just walked away and left me for dead.

What do you hold on to when there's nothing left to hold onto? But the love of God which is in Jesus Christ Our Lord. Sometimes in life it's

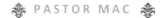

just that real.

Ironically, before it all began to unfold some seven years earlier, my prayer that I taught to my congregation was:" HOLY SPIRIT, LEAD ME AND GUIDE ME INTO ALL TRUTH AND UNDERSTANDING.RESCUE ME FROM ANYTHING OR ANYBODY THAT DOES NOT HAVE MY BEST INTEREST AT HEART. CREATE IN ME A CLEAN HEART AND RENEW A RIGHT SPIRIT IN ME".

Attached to all of my personal texts and emails was this position I took for others as Christ did for me and for us all: "Forgive me for all of the wrong that others have caused in your life. I sincerely apologize". And under my watch, I accept full responsibility for it all but know this; For God I'll still live and for God I'll still die, blessed be the name of the Lord.

I LET G0

HOLD ON AND DIE OR LET GO AND LIVE

Chapter 9

Sermonic Lesson

UNSHAKEABLE FAITH
Romans 8:36-39

In testimony I share why I find myself at this crossroad. In the winter of December 1980, I joined my first church and accepted Jesus as my saving grace, to the glory of God. My relationship, since I met Jesus can simply be defined in Revelation 12:11 " and they overcame him (Satan) by the blood of the lamb, and by the word of their testimony and they loved not their lives unto the death." The song writer and artist Donald Vails confirmed my life in Christ with these words.

Since I met Jesus

There's been a burning... Oh such a burning deep down within.

He holds me with an unseen power. And he turns me away from all my sins.

He changes me from day to day. as I travel along, this old narrow way.

Since I met Jesus... Since He saved this old soul of mine.

It makes me want to run on and shout hallelujah right to the end.

His yoke is easy - his burdens are light.

 I'll walk where he leads me and I'll always be right.

I'll cherish this race and run it with haste.

And by his grace, I know I'll make it home someday.

In my 50-year memoir, 41 years were lived as a Christian. Regrettably, all 50 years were lived amid unimaginable accusations, constant pressure, life-threatening illnesses since birth, disappointment, unforeseen challenges, attacks on my credibility, Integrity, accomplishments and an attempt to convert even my physical nature, but by him, in him and through him I have remained steadfast and unmovable always abounding in the work and spirit of the Lord. I submit to you, that is why I have been attacked so ferociously. I have declared more times than I can remember, even in encouraging myself, that like a tree planted by the waters, I shall not be moved. Many and much has attempted to uproot the decision I made in 1980 but I decided to follow Jesus, with a made-up mind, no turning back. I fell in love with him and what I believed he did for me and I could relate to someone caring for others so much that they would give tirelessly of themselves. It all clicked for me. One of my themes in life, and in survival mode was that "if he was willing to die for me, then I'm willing to live for him." My faith in this man's work and the blood he shed for me has become my DNA. It is the source of my life and strengths. Often referred to as an angel while being treated like an ass. I never thought I should even be compensated for working for such an awesome and Sovereign God. It was my reasonable service. I was hurt all the time, especially during my 15 years as a pastor. Taunted, disrespected and used. I even felt crucified for doing good. I tolerated and accepted it all as my duty and honor to suffer for and by others as He suffered for me. Make no mistake going forward. My DNA is the same but how I process the blood has changed. Boy have I learned a lesson. I am not Jesus. I've lost everything many times over. However, I stand with Jesus as Ruth stood with Naomi when her husband Boaz died, and her mother-in-law tried to send her away to find another man to bring her happiness. Ruth said don't urge me to leave you or to turn back from you. Where you go, I'll go. Where you stay, I will stay. Your people will be my people. I've attempted much and gained little. Tried to fly with oil on my wings. Rise up with weights on my back. Climb steep stairs with no handrails to balance me. I've tried to sing the Lord's song In a Strange Land. But today I still decree like Job, for God I'll live and for God I'll die. Blessed be the name of the Lord.

How do you feel? Where is your faith? Have you been tried and tested? Are you for real or are you a fake replica that looks real? Whether you are a Christian or simply traveling this road of life, is there one thing that you made up your mind about, and stood on, never wavered from or backed down no matter how severe and consistently you've been attacked or by whom? If you had to choose one word or thought that totally embraced your position of faith and works in Christ, what would that be? Family friend or Foe, how often has your foundation or beliefs been shattered but something compelled you to rest for a moment, rise to the occasion and restart your engine and return to flight. As for me, the living Bible version of Romans 8:36 to 39 is my template for life. No, for the scriptures tell us that for his sake we must be ready to face death at every moment of the day. We are like sheep awaiting Slaughter. But despite all this, overwhelming Victory Is Ours through Christ who loved us enough to die for us. For I am convinced that nothing can ever separate me from his love. Death can't, and life can't. The Angels won't, and all the powers of Hell itself can't keep God's love away. Our fears for today, our worries about tomorrow, or where we are – high above the sky or in the deepest ocean - nothing will ever be able to separate us from the love of God demonstrated by our Lord Jesus Christ when he died for us.

Unshakeable Faith……. IT'S A DONE DEAL

Unshakeable Faith……. IT'S A WRAP

Unshakeable Faith…….IS……. CASE DISMISSED

CONCLUSION

This 50-year Memoir is my story. This is my story. This is my song. I'm praising my savior, all the day long. The cover of this book is reflective of those 50 years; the bright array of colors reflects the sunshine(son). the light that shineth out in darkness. The purple represents royalty. For I am fearfully and wonderfully made and a royal priesthood. And the beauty and joy I found serving the man that gave me purpose, direction and unconditional love. The cross that I hung on and with him with pride. It represents the years I spent in vanity and pride. Caring not my Lord was crucified. Knowing it was for me he died at Calvary. Mercy there was great, and Grace was free. Pardon there was multiplied to me. There my burdened soul found Liberty, at Calvary.

The nine Birds around the steps reflect the nine times I tried to soar, fly and rise above to the top of that ladder to bring glory to the one that is hanging on that cross. On this journey I have lost everybody many times. I have lost everything many times. I have had to start all over again many times. By Him and in Him I live and have my being and because of Him I have suffered for the sake of that cross. I started this 50-year journey at the age of 16 and here I am now at age 66, starting all over again. The number 50 according to the study of numerology, means personal freedom.

As I write this Memoir, I am free. Praise the Lord, I'm free. No longer bound. No one's chains holding me. My soul is resting. It's just a blessing. Praise the Lord, hallelujah, I'm free. Fifty Is the pursuit of whatever may be of interest, at the moment it becomes of interest, without resistance from its inner self or from others. I don't know what the future holds but I know who holds the future for me. While I lifted off on every occasion, I never could rise high enough to soar, but every day I woke up, I found myself on the runway trying to go somewhere. Reaching for greater. Pressing toward the mark of the High Calling of God in Christ Jesus. Starting all over again at 66 with a GED educational level could be a bit frightening, but I am numb to disappointment.

I will love my Jesus forever and will never give up on the fact that somehow, someway, somewhere, someday, with his eyes watching over me, directing me, covering and keeping me, I'll rise. Starting a business, getting married or fully engaging in or starting a church all represents failure, but there is one thing I didn't fail at and that was loving Christ and his work to a fault, and when and if he calls me again, I will answer. I'll be somewhere listening for my name.

I surmise in my humanity that the storms of 1980 (my first church), 2018 (my third wife and church), and 1988 (my third business), Took a serious toll on my credibility, the stigma attached to my name, and desire to re-energize. The constant attacks were discouraging, evident and systemic. I don't know if the pattern that my life has taken is interrupted at this point or if what seems to be a curse is broken. I mean, what do you do when what you love most and desire to do most is twisted and tainted and your purpose for living is crushed and severely stained? I do know that the truth has been revealed and I'm still confident that in due season, I will reap if I faint not. I do know that when peace like a river, attendeth my way. When sorrows like sea billows roar. Whatever my lot, thou have taught me to say. It is well, it Is well, with my soul. Under normal circumstances we are encouraged to hold on. Don't give up. Hang on in there. Don't throw in the towel. In context, never give up on God, for God never gives up on you. Yes, hold on, but not to the extent that it is suppressing and destroying your desire, God's Will and purpose for your life. If it does not compliment, support and enhance the quality of your life in some form, it is not of God. God only wants what's best for you. do not be deceived. Every good and perfect gift comes from God. If it's of and from God it will last, and if it's not it will soon fade away. Holding on to things or people that are not pertinent to your cause or calling serves you no good or worthy significance. It drains you of valuable time, energy, resources and is useless and not in the will of God for your life. They are symptomatic of a toxic conclusion. Perspective is key and can subvert or undermine your direction and focus. Accepting, tolerating and clinging to a hot coal that's burning and causing you discomfort and permanent scars that don't heal is not in God's will for your life. Holding on to people, places and things excessively, and are out of season and for the wrong reason can cripple your growth and development. Everybody is not meant to be in your life all the time. They are sent and or come for a purpose and it's essential to know when that purpose is ended. Things and technology are constantly changing to complement and compensate for your continued advancement in your purpose. Always be ready to shift and change accordingly to accommodate your next level. Say thank you and goodbye. Nothing and no one last forever. Start conditioning yourself for the departure of some old stuff and the induction of some new era necessities.

Because of our love, devotion and compassion for others, our hearts can operate out of balance, restraint or vision. It doesn't know when and how to stop, recognize and shift levels. Because of God's unconditional love for us we often feel compelled to pour out, give and reciprocate. But there must be balance in all we do for perfection and productivity to occur. Yes, hold on to God's unchanging hands. Hold on to hope. Hold on to those things that Inspire, enlighten, sustain, strengthen, and enhance the quality of our lives and not deplete, deteriorate and diminish us in quantity and quality. Hold on to those things that increase you and gives you the power to get wealth and not sift you and depreciate you in value, peace and abundance. Hold on to people that add to not constantly take away from. Every moment you spend entangled in others' webs is an abuse of your divinely allotted time to make your mark on this Earth. Through your family or business, your church or in your community. Things, people and situations that are not yours. They don't belong to you. God did not place them in your pathway or purpose. They are not a part of your test or your testimony. Your name is not attached to them or they're only there for a season. Remember, when God gives you an assignment, there are usually some instructions attached or, some resources provided and some people designated to help you fulfill your mission. Ask the Holy Spirit to teach you how to distinguish who and what. He does not put you on a journey without a map or a GPS. In the old American Express way," don't leave home without him". He doesn't lead us into the dark, he guides us through the dark. learn how to distinguish who and what they are, thank them and let them go. Stop letting them consume, confuse and Conquer you. Stop letting them distract, deprive and delay your mission. Your time is of the essence and is very valuable. They eat out at your life and weigh you down.

Your contributions in life, your gifts and your talents can only be effective or realized in this ever-evolving universe when you fulfill that which you have been assigned by using the gifts God gave you, to do it. Often, at the closing of our journey here, we can clearly reflect on what we did for everybody else. Or what everybody else wanted us to do for them. Your eulogy should read how you lived and fulfilled your mandate as God gave it to you or as you chose. That's when, how and where we change history, and enhance the Kingdom of Heaven on Earth. Your life should be a portrait of his glory through your successes. Let your light so shine that the men will see your good works and bring Glory not only to God but to the world in which you live and thrive, and an example to your parents, your children and your loved ones. Your legacy should take on life form. Who are you? What were you sent here to do? Find that answer. Diligently seek for it and in that you can begin to identify with what to hold onto and what to let go of. All too often I did what everyone wanted and needed and thought I should, and it didn't even matter in the end. Be strategic, focused, purpose driven and expectant of results with your talents, your contributions and your sacrifices.

The fact is, in every chapter or era in my life I have asked many who worked against me and turned on me or disliked me a question. What have I done to you to deserve how you accept and treat me? To this day, no one has been able to answer me. That's sad. Very sad. Don't go through life hating on people, when the only explanation you can give them is", I don't know it's just something about you," or because of what somebody else had to say. If you really had to hate, dislike or disrespect someone, please have some resemblance of a reason that you experienced on your own. Blessings that are often sent our way are rejected because of our ignorance. The question in your life should be, is what I have done and who I have been, what God established in my life and path, or was it influenced by something else. Doing you can never make me happy. Trust me, the day will come when you will question yourself about How life would have been if I had done what I really wanted to in my heart. Try starting today to press toward a higher Mark, a greater goal because it is only in that self-fulfillment and the work that you do for Christ that will bring ultimate peace, Joy contentment and a productive life. Don't let the closing statement of your journey be one of stress and pressure because I did everything but what I wanted and what I believed God wanted. Break that curse and tear down those strongholds over your life. Maya Angelou stated that, I love you and I don't mind helping you if I can, but your issues are yours and not mine. People treat you like their fate is your fault. Everyone must bear his own cross, own his own choices, and endure the consequences thereof. Carrying your weight will hinder me from balancing my own with perfection, productivity and perseverance.

Your gifts, talents, calling and visions are what will change the course of history. For God placed every member in the body (Church) as it pleased him, to contribute according to that which we have been assigned to change this world. We are compacted (empowered)by that which every joint (member) supplies (bring) to the table. From almost the very beginning of creation, pain and suffering became the curse (punishment) and they are essential elements to growth and development. Because of my love for Christ and what he did for me, I carried many, circumvented many struggles, slowed down the process and punishment for bad judgment. I may have loved people to their own detriment, believing that it was required of Me by God, and I suffered loss at every turn. All of us must face our own fears and confront our own challenges in life. I'm willing to own and face that possibility and change it now. Can you imagine the words on my tombstone? He went to hell because he loved Heaven too much. We're usually hurt most by the people we love most.

The Bible teaches in Matthews 4:4, that all things should be done in moderation. I can extract from this that too much of anything can be harmful, damaging and can have an adverse effect. I admit I gave too much and for too long. I loved too hard and it became a heavy burden that I thought I was managing to the glory of God through my devoted work for Jesus. My ongoing love and constant sacrifices sent the wrong signal and simply resulted in a dependence upon me to carry people through their issues and not allow them to stand on their own two feet. Figuratively speaking. A serious misconception by me had now become an expectation of me and when I could no longer fulfill their many needs, they abandoned me. From church members to family members. Trampling on my heart was a norm and it was killing me. They began to rely on my compassion and love for God's children while exercising no serious actions or intent to correct and change their ways. They became comfortable, complacent and content and as an added weight for me to carry. There must be measure and balance against every decision and action that we engage in. An intended strategy for correction and improvement or all of our work is in vain. You've got to know when to hold them and know when to fold them. Know that when your giving and pouring into the lives of others is being interrupted as a responsibility or expectation it will leave you bearing someone's cross and ending up accepting the full weight of their issues. Yes, I am saying that even God's love has to be measured and distributed effectively and according to its assigned purpose to create change. Unconditional love was exemplified and demonstrated on the cross with conditions. John 3:16 declares this fact to be that for God so loved the world that he gave his all (only begotten son) that whosoever believeth in him should not perish but have everlasting life. His love was designed and targeted to accomplish at least two major issues. Death and unbearable suffering and to secure eternal life. Even unconditional love must be exemplified with purpose and an expected end. Not because you're just supposed to do it. That's when it becomes an unproductive and unnecessary weight to the giver and a danger to who you are assigned to give it. Your sacrifices are expected and required to serve a useful purpose, not to satisfy some personal gratification or expectation of someone else. If you really want it, God's got it. Jesus's sacrifices for us were for a strategic purpose and demonstrated with a strategic plan of action.

His love and sacrifices and mine as his under shepherd required something from the recipient. Was his death in vain? Was my work in vain? For 41 years, I held on to the desires of my heart to please God and carry out the mandate of the cross. Only to end up hurt and used more by those I helped, and at every turn it seemed that my passion for his people was selfishly sought and my burdens multiplied. We must learn how to detect when our love and commitment is not received, Shake the Dust and redirect our energies so that our work is not in vain and the quality and the substance of our lives are not drained and depleted. For we were all promised an abundant life, liberty and the pursuit of happiness and given gifts and talents to meet that end. I am damaged goods. but because of the consistent flow of the blood of Jesus, I've been made whole. After 50 years, I got it. I've learned what to hold on to and what to let go of. And moreover, I've learned how to do both. Long before I acknowledged Christ as my Saving Grace, like Jeremiah, he knew me and inspired in me a genuine love for his children and and unquestionable gratitude for my mama and my will to show her through my life, her value as a human being in spite of the devastating pain and suffering she was subjected to. This love that I possess is in my DNA and it has driven me for 50 years.

As I shared with you in the beginning, my deep abiding love for Jesus and my mama has dominated my journey and purpose for living. With all that is within me and my nine attempts to soar for their pleasure and Glory, I dedicate my life and this 50-year disclosure to Jesus Christ, son of the Living God, and Annie Bell McLaurin, my mama. On June 17, 2021, while I walked by the poolside in Jamaica, I was called and informed of the medical prognosis that my mother's heart would fail her in less than one year. Such is the continuation of my life's pattern. Even in honoring and celebrating her life, I am reminded of her death. My end is not yet death. God willing. But the mention of hers nearing, is killing me softly. For the first two or three days of my vacation, I was subsequently visited by her many life experiences. I watched her wear the title of " bitch " on every visit to her mother in North Carolina when she cared more and did more for her than her eight siblings. I know where every mark on her body is from the brutal beatings by her alcoholic husband. I was reminded of all of the extremely selfish and ungrateful acts against her by her own children and grandchildren. Their blatant disrespect, disregard and insensitivity for her privacy, her person or her property by her children. The outside affair of my father and the child that resulted. The ensnares and deceptive tactics instituted by her children. The threats on my life if I visited her or moved into her home to care for her and the snakes that I truly hate as much as I do Satan, the serpent that deceptively contributed to the fall of Man ,God's creation, that they planted in her home to keep me away. I was reminded of her mice infested home and how they paraded around her feet at night while she watched TV to the point that she had to prop her feet up off the floor. Trying to hold on when there's nothing to grab hold to or there's nothing that's even salvageable.

From my mother, Jesus my Savior, and I after 50 years of uninterrupted attacks on my life, I impart this message to you. It's easy to say" I love you "when there's nothing required of you on my behalf. Love is an action word. True love is put to the test when it's time to reciprocate. give back. Stretch. Reach Out. when it's time to give in any capacity, your time, money or forfeiting something of great need and value to you. What's Love Got to Do with It, when you're only there for me as long as I don't need anything from you. Those words, I love you are cute and sound good but today are becoming a part of a standard greeting. Hey! hugs and kisses! Love you! holla! have a good one! An action word with no emotional attachment. Just a kind gesture that's not backed by or attached to an experience or encounter. It's a word that embodies the greatest act of humankind. For God so loved that He gave. Love gives. Love's acts. Love sacrifices. It's a term that is often used to appease one's guilt. Can you love me when I'm in the trenches of life and my needs require you to step out of your comfort and into the painful reality of my storm?

For all of my mother's adult life, and in particular the last 20 years, this has been her fate and return on her love by those who she cared for the most. Abuse me. Use me. Cut me. And bruise me and frame it with love. Show me sometimes even a little love and you won't have to say it as much. Action speaks louder than words. Love is responsive. That is acting quickly and positively with interest and enthusiasm. Everybody says and reacts to I love you. With words. But love must be measured and followed with acts of reciprocation. There is a portrait of Jesus hanging on the cross with thorns on his head, pierced in his side, nailed to a cross. Someone asked Jesus, ``How much do you love me? "He said this much. And he hung his head and died. We are taught that we should love not only in words, but in action (deeds). God taught us that we should exemplify our love for him in even loving our enemies. True, genuine love must be measured and reciprocated. John 21:15 -17. Jesus asked Peter three times, Peter, do you love me? Irritating him each time and the third time he asked, Peter, if you really mean it, if you are telling the truth, if you are willing to prove it, feed my sheep. Try measuring your mother's love and apply an action to it. Talk is cheap and even God frowns on its emptiness. Put up or shut up. And do it while she's alive. After all, the Final Act of Jesus on the cross before he died was giving his mother a son to replace her loss. "That's What Love's Got To Do With It." By the way, in case I didn't mention it. I have scars on my body like my mother to reflect the weaknesses and infirmities of others. I possess her same struggles and disappointments in my life. I have the same front tooth missing. I have arthritis in the same hand and on the same finger as she does. And I have the same swollen right ankle, high blood and diabetes as she does. And I have the same ability and the desire despite my circumstances to love Jesus now more than ever before.

Her mental capacity is now overwhelmed by dementia. such an ugly illness whose cure has not yet been dispatched from heaven. And it's most disappointing to me that even if she reads these words, she may not remember the life attached to them. And even if she holds this 50-year Memoir of her son's life in her hand, there may be no recollection of his constant battle. And because of all of the pain and disappointment inflicted upon her person for 70 years, maybe that's a good thing. As Jesus taught, I'm trying to give thanks in all things. For this is the will of God in Christ Jesus. I am confident that many of you whose love for Jesus and compassionate heart for humankind has created many challenges in your life. Mine I am sure are not isolated. Writing this 50-year memoir was sensitive, personal and graphic. It is a simple assessment of my life and experiences. While it can serve as educational, spiritual, psychological, philosophical or an advantageous resource, it is not backed by any standards of professional or documented studies or conclusions and proven criteria. Except as it pertains to God's Living Word.

The Bible. It is simply my life as I was led or chose to live it and the consequences that resulted thereof. However, I am able to substantiate a dominant portion of its content. For all involved whose names are not here to attached or revealed, The Bible says that they shall know the truth, and the truth shall make them free. My life has been a mystery of ongoing failures nine times and internal battles. Three businesses I started. three marriages I've allowed. Three churches I attended. There has been no reconciliation on my part or my opposers, and it seems unlikely at this time. At the end of every failure, every situation, personal or corporate, I was told that it was all my fault, I caused it all and deserved to suffer loss. I was simply left in the ditch bleeding profusely and forgotten that I ever existed.

Be that as it may. I'm reminded of my daddy's favorite gospel hymn. If I can help somebody, as I pass along. If I can cheer somebody with a word or a song. If I can tell somebody that they're traveling wrong. Then my living shall not be in vain. As an added focus, I developed a tool or a measurement that forms my character and keeps me aligned with my spirit and work for Christ. It is collectively personified by Malcolm, Martin, Jesus, my mama, and the Office of the President. With the combination of those spirits you can always count on my best performance. I invite you to make the contrast. Commitment to cause, suffering, fighting for others, unconditional love and an appreciation for life. I don't know what else is going to be required of me, but to date, I've given my best and I've given all I had to give. In many cases and places where it was not my responsibility to do so.

I write this book in hopes that you may triumph in my failures. That the things that I have learned, observed and experienced, even in pain and failure will enlighten, inspire, expose, encourage and change the undesired or undeserved path you may be on. We all have a duty to enhance the kingdom of God on Earth or contribute to the growth and development of a local and Global democracy. On a small or large-scale, all of our contributions matter. We all have a Duty or a mission. We all have gifts, talents, callings and assignments to help fulfill this mandate that is a right and privilege by citizenship. Opportunity is available and God has promised in doing so that we can have a life of abundance, Joy, peace, and prosperity. Sometimes traps are set for our failures. Obstacles and strongholds are placed in our path. We hold on to people that serve no purpose too long. They drain us and benefit us no gain in our Pursuit. We hold on to things that hold us back and weigh us down. People that clearly don't have our best interest at heart. We Fear starting over again when we fall. We are scared of failure and thereby incarcerated by fear. Our self-esteem is low, and we let the wrong people suffocate us and drain our energy. Deplete our resources. Deteriorate Us in value, substance and a sense of importance and ultimately diminish the quality of life that God wants and established even in the beginning. His promises are still available and within reach for all of us. We become depressed, suppressed and crippled in our ability to perform and produce results. Oil on our wings, weighing us down so that we can't rise above our present. These issues are killing us financially, socially, psychologically and destroying our witness. They are destroying our dreams, vision and causing our God-given abilities to be of no effect. We hold onto stuff and people because of guilt, loneliness and debt. God wants us to be free to live out the true purpose of Our Lives and enjoy this journey to life liberty and the pursuit of happiness.

My prayer is that anything, anybody, any experience, teaching or philosophy that's working against the path that God has placed you on.

Any desire of your heart to accomplish, that my life experiences, and all of its disappointment and mystery will compel you to consider in every area of your lives whether to:

HOLD ON AND DIE OR LET GO AND LIVE

Release that hot coal. Stop justifying and excusing why you should keep holding on to it. It's not only burning and hurting you. It's causing permanent, irreparable damage. Let it go now, so the healing can begin.

Get up every day focused and give life all you got and let the chips, people and their stuff fall where it may. Hold on to what works for you and let go of what doesn't.

This is Pastor Mac. This is my story and I'm sticking to it.

Though he slay me, yet will I trust him. For God I'll still live, and for God I'll still die. Blessed be the name of the Lord.

PEACE OUT

ABOUT THE
AUTHOR

Pastor Arnold McLaurin was born in Manhattan, New York in 1955. He was told by his mother that his compassionate care for people was revealed at the tender age of twelve. Pastor McLaurin moved to Washington, D.C. in 1964 and having experienced the plight of God's people in D.C., MD, and VA., he was inspired to respond to Heaven's need to "Feed My Sheep."

He is the third oldest of eight siblings and at the age of four returned to his family's birth place in Snow Hill, North Carolina. The Great, Great Grandson of a slave from the plantation of an Irish Slave Master in Wilmington, North Carolina named McLaurin, migrated to Washington, D. C. in 1964 just prior to the devastation of the King Riots.

Pastor McLaurin attended Cardozo High School in Washington, D.C. just prior to joining the USAF (United States Air Force) in 1971 at the age of seventeen where he received his GED. He has been an entrepreneur and self-employed most of his adult life. Developed in the philosophy of "learning by experience" or more eloquently referred to as "on the job training" which he took pride in being the manager at the Peoples Drug Store from 1976-1980.

He was mandated by choice to live on the principle that "If I don't produce then I don't eat!" He also Founded and Incorporated three businesses, one as a thirty-eight year "Cabbie" in the District of Columbia. He has been married three times and now divorced, a devoted member of three churches, serving the first church for twenty years and the second church as an Associate Minister for four years. The third he founded and pastored for fifteen years. Sold out on the life and doctrine of Jesus Christ and Him crucified since the winter of 1980.

Favorite Scripture Matthews 18:19-20: "Again, I say unto you, that if two of you shall agree on earth as touching anything that they shall ask, it shall be done for them of my Father which is in heaven. For where two or three are gathered together in my name, there am I in the midst of them."

Please feel free to contact Pastor Arnold McLaurin (Pastor Mac) with comments or questions at P. O. Box 56332, Washington, DC 20040 and by email at REVmclaurin@aol.com.

Printed in Great Britain
by Amazon